THE HANGING GARDENS OF THUNDER RIVER

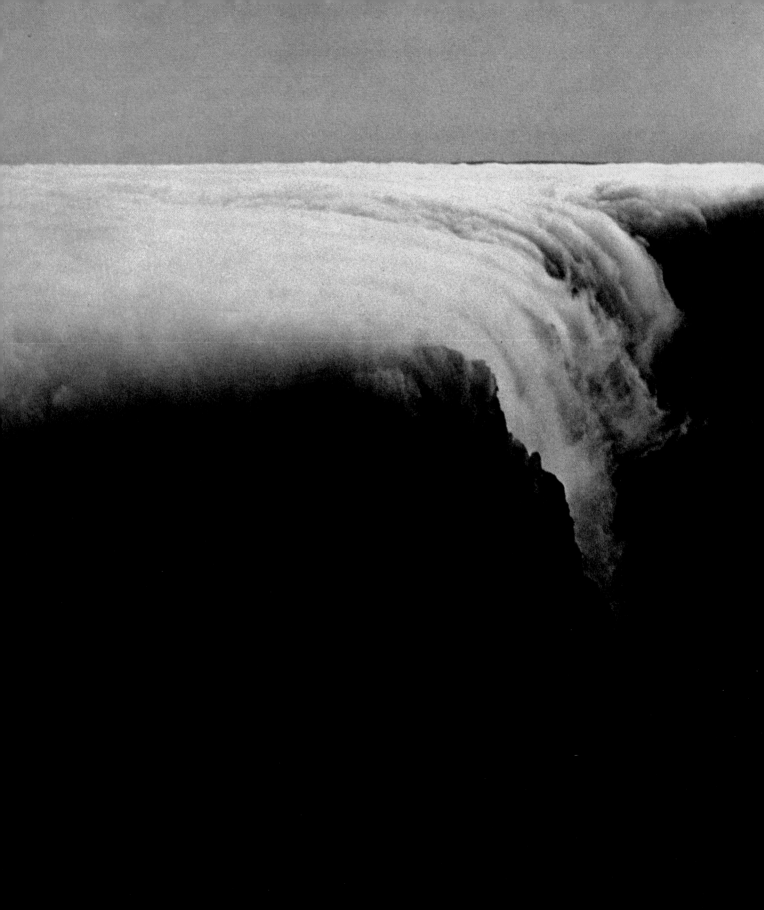

FOG ON THE CANYON RIM

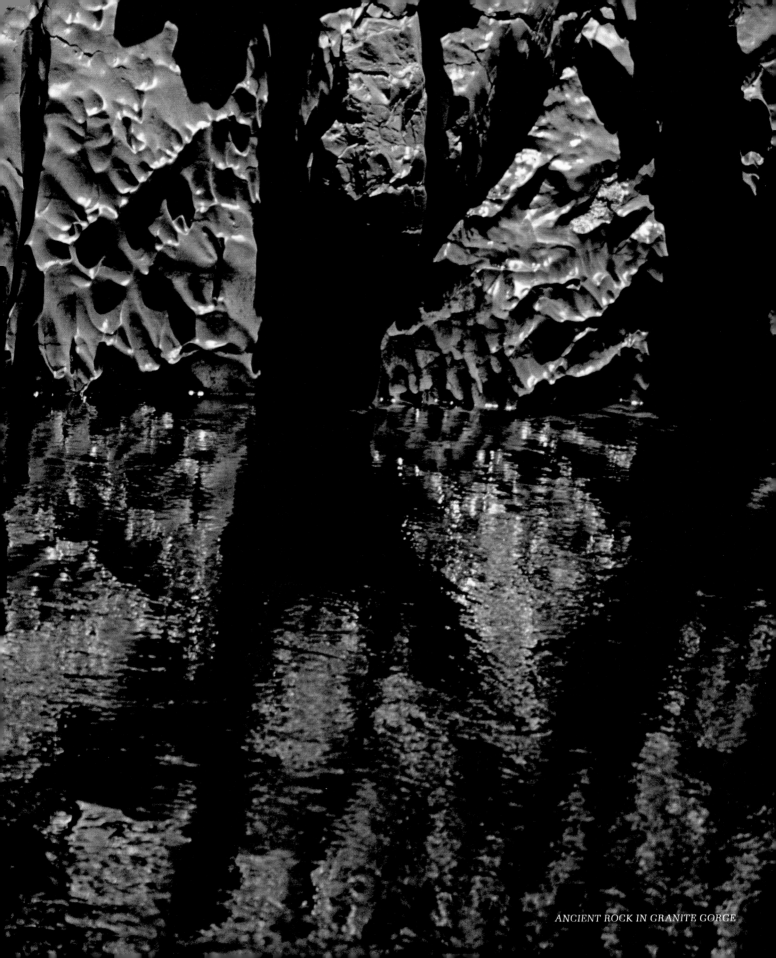

ANCIENT ROCK IN GRANITE GORGE

A BEND OF THE COLORADO RIVER

AN AUTUMN STORM

LIFE WORLD LIBRARY
LIFE NATURE LIBRARY
TIME READING PROGRAM
THE LIFE HISTORY OF THE UNITED STATES
LIFE SCIENCE LIBRARY
GREAT AGES OF MAN
TIME-LIFE LIBRARY OF ART
TIME-LIFE LIBRARY OF AMERICA
FOODS OF THE WORLD
THIS FABULOUS CENTURY
LIFE LIBRARY OF PHOTOGRAPHY
THE TIME-LIFE ENCYCLOPEDIA OF GARDENING
FAMILY LIBRARY
   THE TIME-LIFE BOOK OF FAMILY FINANCE
   THE TIME-LIFE FAMILY LEGAL GUIDE
THE AMERICAN WILDERNESS

THE GRAND CANYON

THE AMERICAN WILDERNESS/TIME-LIFE BOOKS/NEW YORK

BY ROBERT WALLACE
AND THE EDITORS OF TIME-LIFE BOOKS

WITH PHOTOGRAPHS BY ERNST HAAS

THE AMERICAN WILDERNESS
Series Editor: Charles Osborne

Editorial Staff for The Grand Canyon:
Text Editor: L. Robert Tschirky
Picture Editor: Iris Friedlander
Designer: Charles Mikolaycak
Staff Writers: Gerald Simons,
Betsy Frankel
Chief Researcher: Martha T. Goolrick
Researchers: Margo Dryden,
Villette Harris, Michael Luftman,
Myra Mangan, Ruth Silva,
Timberlake Wertenbaker
Design Assistant: Mervyn Clay

Editorial Production
Production Editor: Douglas B. Graham
Quality Director: Robert L. Young
Assistant: James J. Cox
Copy Staff: Rosalind Stubenberg,
Eleanore W. Karsten, Florence Keith
Picture Department: Dolores A. Littles,
Joan Lynch

Valuable assistance was given by the
following departments and individuals
of Time Inc.: Editorial Production, Nor-
man Airey, Margaret T. Fischer; Library, Peter Draz; Picture Collection,
Doris O'Neil; Photographic Laboratory,
George Karas; TIME-LIFE News Service,
Murray J. Gart.

The Author: Robert Wallace, a staff writer for TIME-LIFE BOOKS, has published more than 100 nonfiction articles as well as numerous poems and short stories. He is the author of five previous TIME-LIFE books: The Rise of Russia in the Great Ages of Man series and, in the Library of Art, The World of Leonardo, The World of Rembrandt, The World of Van Gogh and The World of Bernini. In preparing for the present volume he made four long visits to the Grand Canyon, including a voyage in a small wooden boat through the Canyon on the Colorado River.

The Consultant: Martin Litton is a writer, photographer and authority on most of the wild places in the Western Hemisphere. Since his first trip to the Grand Canyon in 1950 he has maintained an active interest in the region.

The Photographer: Ernst Haas, a Vienna-born painter turned photographer, is best known for his dramatic innovations in color photography. He has photographed many major pictorial essays for LIFE magazine and TIME-LIFE BOOKS, and has summed up his work in nature photography in a book of his own, The Creation.

The Cover: A fiery sunrise in the Grand Canyon silhouettes the North Rim (left), the flat-topped bulk of Wotan's Throne (center) and the sharp pinnacle of Vishnu Temple (right). The photograph was taken near Grand Canyon village on the South Rim, which curves to form the horizon at extreme right.

Contents

The Grand Canyon: A Riverside Wilderness

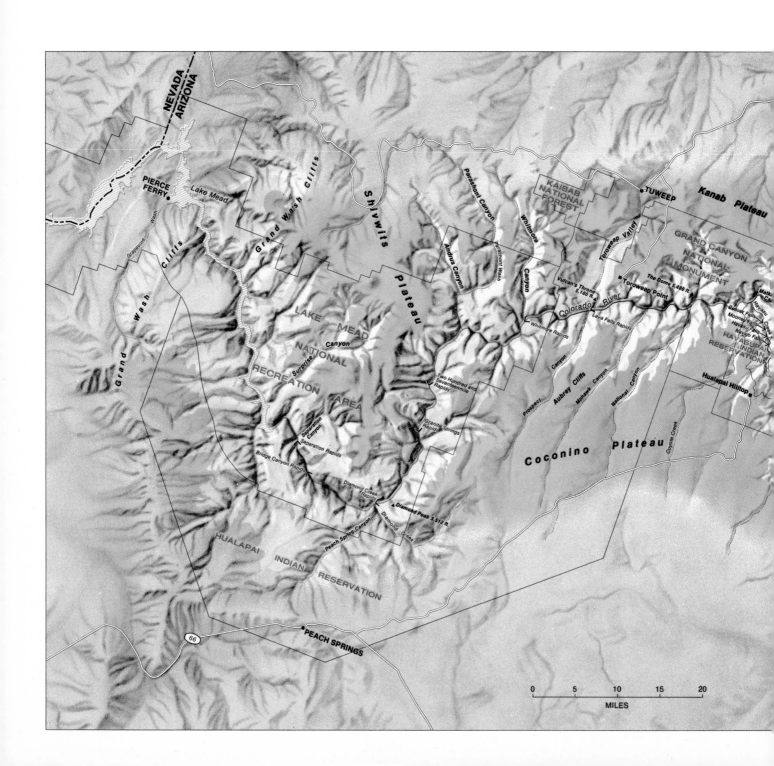

The Grand Canyon region (blue rectangle at right) is detailed in the relief map below, with its wilderness area highlighted in color. The Canyon itself consists of about 2,000 square miles stretched out along 277 miles of the Colorado River, which descends 2,200 feet in that span. The map is labeled with particular reference to features discussed in this book. Red outlines trace the boundaries of the Grand Canyon National Park, national monuments, national forests, Indian reservations and recreation areas; names of these appear in red type. Rivers are shown in blue, with broken blue lines marking stream beds that are dry part of the year; a black "V" across the Colorado indicates rapids. Trails are represented by black lines, roads by double lines and circled numbers, towns by black dots and points of special interest by black squares. Black triangles mark high-altitude points.

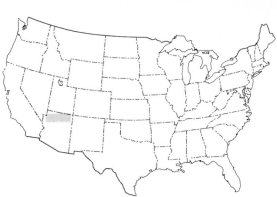

1/ A Wilderness of Stone

The scene is so weird and lonely and so incomprehensible in its novelty that one feels that it could never have been viewed before.

FREDERICK S. DELLENBAUGH/ *THE ROMANCE OF THE COLORADO RIVER*

There is no landscape on earth that is more astonishing than the Grand Canyon of Arizona. When a man first stands on its rim and images of the Canyon flash through his nerves to his mind, the mind reacts like a badly programed computer signaling "input not acceptable" or "reject." Or so at least do the minds of most people except Southwestern Indians, who have been looking at the Grand Canyon for a long time. However, most Americans are of European ancestry and have acquired from their forebears a far different idea of what a landscape should and should not be. It ought to have relatively modest colors and contours. It ought to have some restraint. It ought not to have purple abysses, vermilion cliffs and stone rainbows flinching under a sun that clangs across the sky like a cymbal.

The Grand Canyon is 277 miles long, a mile deep and as much as 18 miles wide. All of it has been carved out by erosion—by the Colorado River and the subtle but overpowering forces of snowflakes, raindrops and air. It is full of precipices, amphitheaters, buttes, slopes, spires, temples and nameless shapes in red, gold, pink, green, rust, orange, mauve and a good many other colors. The shapes within the Canyon, viewed at different times, seem to be moving. At midday they appear to withdraw to the sides, flattening themselves against the many-layered walls as though they feared the sun. Then, as the day dwindles and the light slants, they come marching forth again in a way that made the poet

Carl Sandburg think of divinity: "There goes God with an army of banners." The Grand Canyon is an awesome place and it is a good idea to approach it cautiously, slowly, both in reality and in reading about it. There will be time enough to descend to the bottom, to ride the river in a wooden boat and to talk to the Indians. The stone in the depths, among the oldest on the face of the planet, has been waiting there for two billion years.

Not everyone on the brink of the Canyon thinks of God. Tourists have been going there since the 1880s. An entry in one of the tattered and yellowed guest books of those days reads: "July 12, 1892. This is a warm place. I fainted when I saw that awful-looking canyon. I never wanted a drink so bad in my life. Goodbye. Gertrude B. Stevens." Fear, although not the common reaction, is still felt by quite a few among the two million people who visit the Canyon each year. About 19,000 of them make the journey to the bottom of the Canyon on muleback. It is a safe excursion, frequently made by adults in their sixties and seventies and by children of 12. The mules never slip or jump off the precipices. They are intelligent animals and will not kill themselves to amuse tourists. However, a few tourists do become acutely uneasy, and once in a rare while the guides of the mule train must tie them in the saddle and pack them out of the Canyon like twitching sacks of potatoes.

A more common reaction to the sight of the Grand Canyon is a sudden collapse of expressive faculty. A man's ancestral European ideas of landscape are dealt such a clout that he is unable to say anything —or, at any rate, much. Gifford Pinchot, an articulate man and an ardent early conservationist who was eventually appointed Chief Forester of the United States by his friend, Theodore Roosevelt, took the mule journey in 1891; Roosevelt himself took it in 1911. All that Pinchot could write in the guest book after the trip was, "Time from head of trail to river and back to head of trail, 9 hours and 55 minutes."

Several poets, nonetheless, have avoided Pinchot's predicament and have managed to write extensively of the Canyon. The Englishman Alfred Noyes found that "gigantic walls of rock,/ Sheer as the world's end, seemed to float in air/ Over the hollows of space, and change their forms/ Like soft blue wood-smoke, with each change of light. . . ." Edgar Lee Masters thought of Indians: "Upon its swimming edge/ The first men of America wondering/ Watched how the changing splendors from ledge to ledge,/ To pinnacle from plinth/ Shifted, as if by restless spirits fanned." It was Sandburg, however, who wrote the most and who became the most excited. When he peered into the Canyon he saw:

Battering rams, blind mules, mounted policemen,
trucks hauling caverns of granite, elephants
grappling gorillas in a death strangle, cathedrals,
arenas, platforms, somersaults of telescoped railroad
train wrecks, exhausted eggheads, piles of skulls,
mountains of empty sockets, mummies of kings and mobs,
memories of work gangs and wrecking crews,
sobs of wind and water storms, all frozen and held
on paths leading on to spirals of new zigzags. . . .

Other observers do not see all of those things or perhaps any of them, but it is true that the first sight of the Grand Canyon is a shock, and that the mind shudders for a while thereafter. The shock is made even greater by the circumstance that one cannot see the Canyon while approaching it. Travelers to Grand Canyon National Park generally drive up to the Canyon itself from the south, many of them along the road from Williams, Arizona. The road ascends the high, gently rising Coconino Plateau—the South Rim of the Grand Canyon is at an elevation of 7,000 feet—through a forest of piñon, juniper, ponderosa pine and scattered Gambel oak. One may sense the presence of the Canyon in the way one may sometimes sense the ocean just over the horizon, but there is no glimpse of it. If the road is deserted, as it may be at dawn, it is worthwhile to stop and listen for a few moments. There is a tremendous quiet up ahead, not merely the expected quiet of very early morning but the brooding, almost supernatural sort of quiet in which an old dog for no apparent reason will whimper.

The trees press close to the road as though asking to be looked at. After the visitor reaches the Canyon he may not bother to look at trees any more, but he should pause here. These are interesting trees. The Gambel oak is a curiosity to those who know the lofty, great-girthed oaks of lower and better-watered regions. In leaf, bark and configuration it resembles its close cousin, the Oregon white oak, but it is dwarfed and in the neighborhood of the Canyon it grows only about 15 feet tall. In order to survive in its high, dry habitat it has developed a communal life: its roots spread horizontally and at intervals shoots arise to form new trees. A grove of Gambel oak may thus appear to consist of 30 or 40 well-spaced, independent individuals but they are all holding hands under the blanket; their roots are interconnected.

Ponderosas have tall, massive orange trunks. Their bark smells like vanilla and their pale yellow wood is soft but strong. It can be cut easily and crisply; the grain is straight and the chips, shavings and sawdust have a fine resinous fragrance. A few whiffs of it can intoxicate an ordinary handyman, making him hope that he can become a master carpenter. It is a sensual pleasure to shape this great wood with hand-sharpened chisels and planes. Ponderosas are extensively logged in the high country of the West above 6,000 feet, but those near the Grand Canyon, part of the Kaibab National Forest, are well guarded. They can be harvested by private companies only after the issuance of a government permit that stipulates which trees may be cut.

Piñon pines appear dwarfed, twisted and straggly beside the great ponderosa, but from an Indian's point of view they are far superior. Curved piñon logs can be used in building huts and hogans; piñon pitch serves as a dressing for wounds, as glue and as a waterproof coating for woven baskets, which thus become bottles. The most important service of the piñon, however, is to provide food. Its cones are filled with brown seeds about the size of small peanuts, which are delicious and have high nutritional value. Many frontiersmen and Indians have been saved from starvation by piñon seeds. Today the seeds are sold in gourmet food stores across the country as "pine nuts" or "Indian nuts."

Junipers, also short and gnarled, grow alongside the piñons and are almost as useful. Their stringy bark makes excellent tinder for lighting fires and can be woven into soft sleeping mats. Their bluish-white berries, which are actually modified cones, can be eaten in an emergency and are nourishing, although a trifle puckery. Many of the junipers near the Canyon, and other evergreens as well, are infested with mistletoe. The plant is parasitical; it sends sucker roots through the bark of the junipers and feeds on their sap. Lumbermen detest mistletoe—it can deform trees, making them commercially useless, or indeed kill them. The tough species of mistletoe found at the Canyon is not the tender Christmas kiss-me variety; its leaves are much smaller and look like tiny triangular scales. Birds are very fond of its grayish berries, which are uncommonly sticky. After a meal of them a bird's beak is often covered with gum in which a seed or two may be stuck. When the bird flies to a neighboring tree to wipe its beak the seeds are transferred, and soon the mistletoe sinks roots into the new host. Despite its habits there are those who love the mistletoe. It is the state flower of Oklahoma—but lumbering in Oklahoma is not a major industry.

As a traveler drives into the national park the trees continue to bound his horizon. Still innocent, his view still blocked, he winds through the park until he comes without warning to a place called Mather Point, a mile from the Park headquarters and visitors' base near Bright Angel Lodge. At Mather Point the road swings close to the rim and the trees have been removed. All creation seems to come to an end. There is a low parapet and beyond it lies the abyss.

The first white men to see the Grand Canyon were Spanish soldiers, fortune hunters who reached the brink in the year 1540. In those days the Spaniards had become accustomed to enchantment and miracle. The Aztec treasure that Hernán Cortés had sent home from Mexico two decades earlier had been followed by an even larger Inca treasure that Francisco Pizarro dispatched from Peru. With the treasures came tales, some true, of tawny, coppery Indians who wore bright feathers and knew astronomy, of strange animals and 30-foot constrictor snakes, of pyramids and rich mines of silver and gold. Thus, when the Spaniards in Mexico heard rumors of golden cities somewhere far to the north, they believed them. With a *Vivat Hispania!* and a *Domino Gloria!* Francisco Vázquez de Coronado, a 30-year-old caballero, marched north into the great American desert. With him went about 300 well-armed young Spaniards, their brains baking under their steel helmets, to find and pillage the cities. Cervantes had not yet written *Don Quixote* but the spectacle would have delighted him.

Coronado found only Indian pueblos, not cities, and although they may have appeared golden in the light of the setting sun they were made of clay. However, he discovered the Grand Canyon—or rather, one of his captains did. When Coronado heard Indian reports of a large river lying to his west he dispatched Captain García López de Cárdenas with 25 companions to examine it. The captain's mind, too, was doubtless a little numb from reacting to the remarkable events and discoveries of the past century. Thus the account of the discovery of the Grand Canyon, which Cárdenas gave to a historian who was traveling with Coronado, lacks the excitement that one might expect. The precipices at the rim of the Canyon become merely "banks."

"After they had gone 20 days," Coronado's scribe wrote, "they came to the banks of the river. It seemed to be more than three or four leagues in an air line across to the other bank of the stream that flowed between them. The country was elevated and full of low, twisted pines, very cold, and lying open to the north." (The precise spot where Cárdenas reached the Canyon cannot be determined, but it was on the South Rim. Very likely Cárdenas encountered the South Rim somewhere between Moran Point and Desert View—both about 10 to 12 miles from the North Rim—which is the only area that can be described as "open to the north." Since a league is three miles, Cárdenas' estimate of the distance across the Canyon also fits this location.

"They spent three days on this bank," Coronado's man went on, "looking for a passage down to the river, which looked from above as if the water was six feet across, although the Indians said it was half a league wide. It was impossible to descend [although] the three lightest and most agile men made an attempt to go down . . . and went down until those who were above were unable to keep sight of them."

No further attempt was made to explore the Canyon. Coronado's men wandered on across the Southwest, fighting shabby little battles with Indians, but finding nothing they regarded as valuable. And so in the year of its discovery, 1540, the Grand Canyon and the high plateaus around it were crossed off the list of places in which civilized men might be interested. More than two centuries passed before another white man came to the rim, went part way into the abyss and left a report of it. The second visitor was in search of something he regarded as more valuable than gold; he was a Franciscan missionary hoping to save Indian souls.

Father Francisco Tomás Garcés, whose base was in the mission of San Xavier del Bac near what is now Tucson, Arizona, climbed down into one of the side canyons of the Grand Canyon in 1776. There he found a small tribe of Indians, the Havasupai, who were so hospitable that they treated him to five days of feasting. However, he was unable to convert them. (The Havasupai are still living in the bottom of their canyon and remain largely unconverted to this day.) Father Garcés also skirted the rim of the Grand Canyon itself and looked in dismay "at the sight of the most profound canyons that ever onward continue, and within these flows the Río Colorado." Father Garcés was the first man to refer consistently to the river as the Colorado, which means "red-colored" in Spanish and refers to the bricklike hue of the silt-laden water.

In the next hundred years only a handful of white men—hunters, trappers and, after the United States acquired the Southwest at the end of the war with Mexico, military surveyors—came near the Grand Canyon. One of the surveyors was Lieutenant Edward F. Beale, a naval officer whom the War Department had chosen to explore the Southwestern desert. In 1857 and 1858 Beale surveyed an east-west route just south of the Canyon. It had been Beale's idea to use camels on this exploration; he persuaded Jefferson Davis, Secretary of War, to authorize the purchase of 80 camels in Tunis, Egypt and Smyrna. With their hired

Arab drivers, the camels were landed in Texas in 1856 and driven overland to Fort Defiance, New Mexico Territory, where the survey began.
Confronted with the strangeness of the American desert, canyons and
Indians, all but one of the camel drivers quit. The exception was a bold
Arab, Hadji Ali, whose name could be only approximately pronounced
by Americans as Hi Jolly. (There is a roadside monument to Hi Jolly,
with that spelling, in Quartzsite, Arizona.)

The camels themselves, however, proved effective in Grand Canyon
country—briefly. They carried as much as 1,000 pounds each, plodding
over snow-covered mountains; needing no shoes, they negotiated
stretches of jagged lava rock that other animals could not cross un-
shod. Lieutenant Beale became enthusiastic and predicted that "every
mail route across the continent will be conducted and worked altogether with this economic brute." The military soon asked Congress
for authority to buy no fewer than 1,000 camels, which cost $375 a-
piece. Civilian syndicates and associations were formed to speculate in
camels, and one group actually imported some from China. The scheme
had one basic flaw: though a few camels, properly managed, were useful, camels in quantity were a handful. They were ugly and they smelled
bad; the mere sight or whiff of them stampeded horses and mules. Also,
American mule skinners could not master the trick of loading a half-
ton of supplies on a camel's back so that the load would not fall off
when the going got rough.

While these problems were being considered, the Civil War began
and the Army forgot about camels. After the war no one wanted the
beasts, which were turned loose to fend for themselves; for years they
wandered across the Southwest startling people and frightening mules
out of their wits. In 1875 the state of Nevada passed a law "to prohibit
camels and dromedaries from running at large on or about the public
highways." Eventually both white and Indian hunters, who ate them in
a pinch, wiped the camels out. Lieutenant Beale went on to become
U.S. Minister to Austria-Hungary.

While the Navy's Lieutenant Beale was working his way westward
through the desert, Lieutenant Joseph C. Ives, an Army officer whom
the War Department chose to explore the Colorado, prepared to sail up
the river from its mouth on the Gulf of California to determine how far
it might be navigable. Ives ordered a Philadelphia shipyard to build *Explorer,* a 50-foot stern-wheel steamer. The vessel was tested on the Del-
aware River, disassembled and shipped via Panama to San Francisco

and then to the mouth of the Colorado, where Ives and his men put it to-gether again and set forth. The voyage took two months of backbreaking labor; *Explorer* bucked powerful currents, frequently ran aground on sandbars and had to be towed by her crew with lines from the banks. But in March 1858 Ives steamed into Black Canyon near the site of the present Hoover (Boulder) Dam, 350 river miles from the Colorado's mouth and 78 short of the Grand Canyon.

Ives had stationed a man in the bow with a sounding pole, and as the little vessel bulled its way forward the soundings were encouraging. But then, as Ives wrote, "the *Explorer,* with a stunning crash, brought up abruptly and instantaneously against a sunken rock. For a second the impression was that the cañon had fallen in. The concussion was so violent that the men near the bow were thrown overboard; [I was] pre-cipitated head foremost into the bottom of the boat; the fireman, who was pitching a log into the fire, went halfway in with it; the boiler was thrown out of place; the steam pipe doubled up; the wheel house torn away; and it was expected that the boat would fill and sink instantly." However, *Explorer* remained afloat and the man who had been work-ing the sounding pole in the bow was dragged out of the water. "Lieutenant!" he shouted, "I believe we may have reached the head of navigation! Stop her!"

Lieutenant Ives and some of his men left *Explorer* in Black Canyon and continued overland to the east, paralleling the river along the South Rim of the Grand Canyon—which had not yet acquired its name. Ives referred to it as "the Big Cañon of the Colorado." After a long march he and his men came to the side canyon where Father Garcés had visited the Havasupai Indians in 1776. Ives's description of the trail into the canyon reads, in part: "It seemed as though a mountain goat could scarcely keep its footing upon the slight indentation that appeared like a thread attached to the rocky wall. . . . I rode upon it first, and the rest of the party and the train followed—one by one—looking very much like a row of insects crawling upon the side of a building. We pro-ceeded for nearly a mile along this singular pathway, which preserved its horizontal direction."

The bottom of the canyon, Ives noted, fell away—in places it dropped a hundred feet at a time—as they rode along it, "till glancing down the side of my mule I found that he was walking within three inches of the brink of a sheer gulf a thousand feet deep; on the other side, nearly touching my knee, was an almost vertical wall rising to an enormous al-titude. The sight made my head swim, and I dismounted and got ahead of the mule, a difficult and delicate operation, which I was thankful to have safely performed. A part of the men became so giddy that they were obliged to creep upon their hands and knees, being unable to walk or stand. . . . A slight deviation in a step would have precipitated one into the frightful abyss."

Lieutenant Ives got safely out of the situation and made his way eastward to such civilization as could be found in 1858 in Fort Defiance. In his report to the War Department he wrote, "Ours has been the first, and will doubtless be the last, party of whites to visit this profitless locality. It seems intended by nature that the Colorado River, along the greater portion of its lonely and majestic way, shall be forever unvisited and undisturbed." The statement appears in several of the histories and guidebooks that are sold in Grand Canyon National Park, where the 60-millionth visitor was due to arrive sometime in the 1970s.

Gloomy though it was, Ives's report contained one positive note: he was the first man in the 318 years since the discovery of the Grand Canyon to speak of its beauty and "majestic" quality. "We paused in wondering delight, surveying this stupendous formation through which the Colorado and its tributaries break their way." Ives had been accompanied by an artist, F. W. von Egloffstein, a Prussian who produced the first sketches of the Canyon. They are nightmarish, almost hallucinatory drawings that might well be used to illustrate passages in Milton or Dante. It may seem surprising that a well-trained artist on a fact-finding mission could have produced such work, but as already noted, the sight of the Canyon can unhinge a man with old established ideas of landscape. Ives himself, a courageous officer not given to morbid fears, sometimes lapsed into prose that is somewhat strong for a government report: "The rapid descent, the increasing magnitude of the colossal piles that blocked the end of the vista, and the corresponding depth and gloom of the gaping chasms into which we were plunging, imparted an unearthly character to a way that might have resembled the portals of the infernal regions."

However fascinated by his account of the Canyon Ives's readers in Washington may have been, the empire builders among them must have felt a pang of disappointment as they scanned the report. It demonstrated, at least to reasonable men, that the Colorado River was navigable only by small boats and over only a small portion of its course. Previously it had been the dream of the empire builders that the Colorado would prove to be another Mississippi, which would serve the Southwest as a great carrier of commerce. But in other regards,

Ives was not able to add a great deal to the tiny sum of knowledge that existed about the Grand Canyon in 1858. The interior of the Canyon, about 2,000 square miles, remained *terra incognita,* the last remaining blank on the map of the United States. To be sure, from the rim of the Canyon—at least, from parts of the rim—one could see the river far below. And in certain places one could *hear* the river, a fact that gave pause to men who knew something about rivers. Rapids that were audible for a distance of one mile would very likely drown anyone who ventured into them.

The Indians were afraid of the river. The Navajo, like many other tribes and nations around the world, had a legend of an ancient flood. In the general inundation their ancestors had escaped drowning by turning into fish—to this day, a religious Navajo will not knowingly or willingly eat fish, lest he be devouring a relative. The waters of the flood, the Navajo assumed, drained away through the bottom of the Grand Canyon. Therefore, he reasoned, there must be a ghastly hole down there into which the river thunders, to run for unknown miles in the depths of the earth. The Indians also believed—quite logically, on the basis of what they could see—that there were high waterfalls between the perpendicular walls of the inner gorge of the Canyon. Men who dared try to navigate the river would be caught in the fierce current, would be unable to reverse direction or climb out, and would inevitably be swept over the falls to death. A good many white men believed much the same thing.

The Grand Canyon remained a blank until 1869, the year of one of the great adventures in the American experience. A one-armed Civil War veteran, Major John Wesley Powell, accompanied by nine men, voyaged down the Colorado from Green River, Wyoming, traveling the entire length of the Canyon in small wooden boats. The trip was a notable triumph: three men died, but not on the river. They were killed by Indians when, unable to face the terrors of the rapids any longer, they said farewell to Powell and climbed out of the Canyon.

Powell took many scientific notes and he demolished the worst of the myths about the Canyon and the river, but he was not a highly trained cartographer. Beautiful topographic maps of Grand Canyon National Park resulted from 20 years of U.S. Geological Survey reconnaissance beginning in 1902, but it was not until 1923 that the survey finally sent an expedition through the Grand Canyon to chart the river itself. The Canyon itself was *still* not completely mapped as late

So powerful is the Grand Canyon's effect on the minds of men that the 19th Century topographer and explorer F. W. von Egloffstein, who illustrated a U.S. Army report on the Colorado River, could produce little more than phantasmic suggestions of a nether world. This engraving was meant to show the canyon at the mouth of Diamond Creek, but the scene is so distorted that no one has been able to identify it with the actual landscape.

as 1971. Aerial stereoscopic photographs had been taken, but final maps of the western parts remained to be published. Moreover there still existed a good many parts of the Canyon where even the lightest and most agile men had never gone—or where, in the old prospector's phrase, the hand of man had never set foot. An accurate and complete biological survey of the Canyon had not yet been made. Some of the towering pinnacles and buttes that rise from the floor of the Canyon had not been climbed. On their flat summits, isolated for a million years or two, life existed—in what bizarre forms, no one knew.

The man leaning over the parapet at Mather Point looking out at the Canyon does not as a rule speculate about strange forms of life, nor is he likely to think of Spaniards in steel helmets or in black robes, of camels, steamboats or the courage of the major with the missing arm —perhaps because of the proximity of parked cars and postcards at Bright Angel Lodge. He merely looks down into the chasm, stunned, and then very soon he becomes aware of the quietness. Not a solitary sound emerges from those depths. It is as though all the silences and hushes of time beyond imagining have drifted into the Canyon and filled it to the brim. During the day, when there is a faint haze in the Canyon, the quietness almost becomes visible; on a deep night on the rim a man can feel a gentle pressure on his eyes and ears as though the silence were reaching up to take hold of him.

In early morning after rain the Canyon may be filled with fog from rim to rim. As the sun climbs higher the fog breaks up into clouds that slowly rise and disappear, and for a brief time the air in the Canyon is clear. Then the sun's rays strike deeper and from the bases of the wet, warming cliffs small new mists come out, join and become fog once more, which rises, breaks up and vanishes in the brightening air. Over and over the process is repeated until all the moisture on the walls is burned away. The dry air within it and above it becomes luminous as light is reflected from the colored cliffs.

The luminosity of the air does not account for the name Bright Angel. Major John Wesley Powell invented the name, which is attached to the tourist lodge, to a transverse geological fault under the Canyon, to a foot and mule trail and to a clear, sparkling creek, a tributary of the Colorado, that enters the Canyon from the north. When Powell and his men made their voyage of exploration they gave names to many previously anonymous things and places. In Utah, making their way in three boats down the Colorado toward the Grand Canyon, they were distressed by the muddiness of the water—it was, in the old vernacular, too thin to plow and too thick to drink. Their hopes were briefly raised when they came to a new stream that flowed into the Colorado from the west. Perhaps it was clear. One of the men in the third boat called out to a man in the first, "How is she?" and got the gloomy reply, "She's a dirty devil." Accordingly Powell dubbed the new river the Dirty Devil, a name it retains despite the efforts of some people to call it the Frémont. The three streams that unite to form the Dirty Devil were called the Starvation, the Muddy and the Stinking.

When Powell reached the Grand Canyon his conscience as a coiner of names may have been pricking him a little. Then, too, he was a literate man and knew the reference in Milton's *Paradise Lost* to "the Angel bright." Thus, after Powell came to a clear creek in the Grand Canyon he compensated for the Dirty Devil by christening the Canyon stream the Bright Angel, and it is from the creek's name that all the other Bright Angels in the neighborhood derive.

On the terrace of Bright Angel Lodge one can often find solitude in midwinter, even though the South Rim remains open all year and the flow of visitors never ceases. (The road to the North Rim is usually blocked by snow from October to May; only one tourist in 10 goes to the North Rim.) In summer, however, the busy terrace on the South Rim is merely a place for a first glance over someone's shoulder. Then by walking a half mile or a mile east or west along the rim one can find all the silence and solitude one wants, to sit against a tree and watch for hours while the Canyon changes in the sun.

The Drama of a Single Day

PHOTOGRAPHS BY HARALD SUND

Not even the most scene-weary visitor fails to look in awe as, minute by minute, his view of Grand Canyon alters before his eyes. In the Canyon landscape, the steadily shifting angle of the sun creates a sequence of contrasts so dramatic that it seems as if the earth itself were experiencing a cosmic adventure that repeats itself each day.

Several factors combine to make the Canyon a uniquely changeable scene. Life seems absent so that nothing vies for attention with the light. Over millions of years, erosion has chiseled or worn the rocks into many angular and rounded striated shapes, each surface reflecting the light and throwing shadows at its own peculiar angle. The light in the Canyon, clear because of the dry air, penetrates the earth to a depth of a mile, revealing 20 layers of rock, each a different color—red shales, yellow-gray limestones, white and brown sandstones, pinkish granite and almost black schists. Flat and soft at noon, when the sun is directly overhead, these colors deepen and intensify in kaleidoscopic variations at other times of day.

The photographs on the following pages are an extraordinary record of a single August day at the Canyon, raising the curtain with the pink, gold and blue colors of sunrise, following the display through the soft brightness of noon and the sudden darkness of an afternoon storm to a rock-reflected sunset. The point of view—the photographer set up his camera at Hopi Point on the Canyon's South Rim—is the same in all of the strikingly different pictures.

6:02 A.M.

8:30 A.M.

12:02 P.M.

3:55 P.M.

4:31 P.M.

6:35 P.M

2/ Two Rims, Two Worlds

There must be few other easily accessible places on earth where it is possible to look into areas never actually explored by man.   JOSEPH WOOD KRUTCH/ GRAND CANYON

Grand Canyon village on the South Rim and Grand Canyon Lodge on the North, the points from which all visitors sooner or later look down into the abyss, are opposite each other and only 10 miles apart. At night their lights wink across the silent space. By day eagles and ravens fly from rim to rim, peering into the gulf for prey or carrion. Clouds and shadows pass. Airborne spores of mushrooms and ferns drift invisibly over the barrier of the Canyon. Scents travel in the wind, the breath of forests of pine and juniper, spruce and fir. In the clear air the rimrock on the other side does not seem remote but closer than 10 miles off, yet to reach it by even the shortest road a man must drive more than 200. For the Grand Canyon is one of the most formidable barriers on earth. It remains only slightly less an obstacle to man today than it was when Captain García López de Cárdenas first laid his Spanish eyes on it in 1540. Even little birds do not as a rule venture to fly straight across. Sparrows and juncos seem uneasy at having a mile of air under them, and when they travel from rim to rim they take it in installments, making many short flights down one side of the Canyon, across the river and up the other side.

There is another more direct way for a man to go from rim to rim: he can hike or ride a mule down into the Canyon along the steep, winding Kaibab Trail and up the trail on the other side. At the bottom of the Kaibab Trail, 65 feet above the river, hangs a contrivance built in 1928 that is wide enough for a man or mule to walk upon and strong enough to support a whole string of mounted tourists. This footbridge contains 67 tons of structural steel, all of which had to be packed down to the river on muleback. It is guyed and supported by eight 1½-inch steel cables. The cables, each 548 feet long and weighing 2,030 pounds, could not be carried down by animals. Accordingly, each cable was unreeled along the South Rim of the Canyon and 50 men, mostly Indians, were lined up beside it at 10- to 12-foot intervals. When the foreman cried "Let's go!" (ma ha! in Havasupai; yeh ta hay! in Navajo) the men shouldered the cable and marched the seven miles down to the river, snaking along the switchbacks like an enormous sidewinder rattlesnake.

Before the construction of the Kaibab Suspension Bridge the river was crossed by an aerial trolley, big enough to hold a man and a mule, that dangled from a wire and was moved by a hand-cranked winch. Theodore Roosevelt and his sons Archie and Quentin, aged 19 and 15, were winched across in 1913 on their way to hunt cougar on the North Rim. Before the trolley there was only a little ferryboat—and that was not located in the Canyon itself but some 37 miles upstream at Lee's Ferry, near today's Navajo Bridge.

Earlier than that there was no way for men to cross the barrier of the Canyon without enormous difficulty, as the Utah-based Saints of the Mormon Church discovered when they hoped to establish a huge state whose boundaries might have extended across the Colorado. The Mormons, who were headquartered at Salt Lake City and also had outposts at Las Vegas, Nevada, and San Bernardino, California, conjectured that the river might eliminate arduous overland journeys and provide a faster route of communication between their various settlements. Under orders from his church, a remarkable man named Jacob Hamblin spent years exploring the region of the Grand Canyon in the 1850s and 1860s, searching for fords and trails. Hamblin, who is called "The Mormon Leatherstocking," came to know that country as well as any man who ever lived. He found crossings of the Colorado at what later became Lee's Ferry and at Grand Wash Cliffs, at the lower end of the Grand Canyon, and often descended into the Canyon itself. He visited the Havasupai living on its floor and learned their language, just as he learned to speak with the Hopi, the Paiutes, the Shivwits and other Indians of the surrounding plateaus. The Indians held him in the utmost respect, as he in turn respected them. He dealt with them by a code that he summed up in one sentence: "Never be angry with an Indian, and always tell him the truth."

Hamblin told the Indians the truth in great things and in small. When he departed from an Indian, intending to return in, say, three weeks, Hamblin would give the Indian a little bag containing 21 beans. "Eat one every sunrise," he would say. "When the last one is gone, I will return," and sure enough, at the end of three weeks Hamblin would come riding over the horizon. Probably no white man in history has been more admired by the red.

Because Hamblin was so esteemed by the Indians, they would have told him whatever secrets they might have kept about the Grand Canyon. If there had been any easy way across it, the Indians undoubtedly would have informed him of it. But there simply is no easy way across the Grand Canyon. For that reason the Mormons never succeeded in establishing much of a foothold south of the Colorado River, although the northwestern corner of Arizona, cut off from the rest of the state by the Grand Canyon, remains Mormon country to this day. It is sometimes called "The Mormon Dixie."

Although the Kaibab Trail bridge spanning the Colorado now makes it possible for the more adventurous tourists and their mounts to travel from rim to rim, the Canyon remains totally unbridgeable to many animals. To biologists the most interesting of these are two squirrels, the Abert on the South Rim and the Kaibab on the North. The Abert and Kaibab squirrels, the handsomest and among the largest of their kind in the United States, were once the same, but they have been separated so long by the barrier of the Canyon that they have evolved into different species. Alike in size, configuration and habits, they are obviously of common ancestry; even the "chuck-chuck" of their bark and their general body color, a dark iron gray with a maroon stripe down the back, are similar. Here the resemblance ends.

The Abert squirrel, which is fairly common in the high pine country of the Southwest, has a white belly and a grayish tail. The Kaibab squirrel, however, has a black belly and a magnificent tail that is almost pure white, a rare tail befitting a rare creature, for the Kaibab squirrel is found nowhere in the world but in a 350-square-mile area adjoining the North Rim of the Grand Canyon. As one drives through the Kaibab National Forest toward the rim it is well worth stopping in hopes of sighting a Kaibab squirrel. They are extremely wary and it takes a keen eye to find them and a telephoto lens to photograph them, but it is delightful to glimpse one going about his business, flourishing his tail like a grandee with a silver cloak.

As to how the processes of evolutionary change may have produced the differences between Kaibab and Abert squirrels, biologists are in somewhat of a quandary. It is at first tempting to conclude that the white tail of the Kaibab has evolved as an aid in camouflaging the squirrel against the snow. The North Rim, being higher than the South Rim, does receive considerably more snow.

But the Kaibab squirrel has an almost black body, as seen against white snow, and does not flip its tail up over its back to conceal itself from a predatory hawk. Instead, it races, tail extended, for the nearest tree. Furthermore the tail is white all year round and is as conspicuous against the brown pine needles in summer as its dark body is against the winter snows. Finally, the difference in belly color—pure white in the Abert and black in the Kaibab—absolutely defies any explanation based on camouflage.

These differences in coloration of the two squirrels, then, may have some adaptive value, but if so it is anything but apparent to biologists at the present time. Perhaps these differences arose by chance, became established in the Kaibab squirrel and, due to its isolation on the North Rim, could not "leak out" to its cousins across the Canyon.

Why do the Abert and Kaibab squirrels not cross the Canyon, interbreed and become one species again? Why are other small mammals and reptiles similarly stranded on the rims? On the North Rim, for example, may be found the long-tailed pocket mouse, the bushy-tailed wood rat and the long-tailed meadow mouse. These, too, are distinct species, resembling but still different from the rock pocket mouse, the Mexican wood rat and the Mexican meadow mouse of the South Rim. Have they followed separate evolutionary paths simply because they could not cope with the Canyon cliffs? Or, if they were capable of climbing up or down the cliffs, were they balked by the ferocious Colorado at the bottom? Studies of their habits and mobility have not yet produced the answers. But in the case of the Abert and Kaibab squirrels the answer is clear.

Both squirrels feed primarily on the twig ends of ponderosa pines. They chew off the twigs a few inches from the terminal buds, peel them and eat the soft, juicy tissue within. Although they occasionally eat the seeds and roots of other plants, the squirrels rely on the pines for their year-round food. They are, in the biologist's word, "tied" to the ponderosa—where the ponderosa cannot live the squirrels cannot live either. Since no ponderosa grows in the arid desert land to the east, west and north of the Canyon or in the warm, dry Canyon itself, the Kaibab squirrel never leaves its 350-square-mile home on the North Rim. The Abert squirrels on the opposite rim can and do range across the Southwest and into parts of northern Mexico, figuratively leaping from pine to pine, but they will not cross the pineless Canyon or the desert to meet and mate with the Kaibabs. These circumstances oblige one to take a broader view of the Canyon as a barrier—it is not only a physical obstacle but a climatological one as well. Its interior weather affects the mobility of animals and plants as much as or even more than its precipices do.

Plants are not the stick-in-the-muds that most people imagine. Actually they are very mobile. Over long periods of time, as geological factors affect their accustomed climate, they can shift across the landscape to more favorable localities. It was because of moving plants—ponderosa—that the Aberts and the Kaibabs were separated. The last glaciers appeared in the Southwest about 20,000 years ago, during what is called the Wisconsin Ice Age, and their presence altered the climate of the Grand Canyon, making it cooler and more humid than it is today. (Glaciers had no role in the *formation* of the Canyon; it had long since been dug by the river.) In the cool moist climate of glacial times, it is thought, ponderosa pines could have grown not only on the rims but deep within the Canyon and east and west of it. The squirrels then had free range. But when the glaciers melted, the interior of the Canyon and the areas east and west became too warm and arid for the ponderosa; slowly the pines withdrew to the high, cool rims and the dependent squirrels followed. Thus they were marooned.

Today several zones of climate exist in the Grand Canyon, forming mini-barriers within the greater barrier of the Canyon itself. Each contains its distinctive forms of plant and animal life, and sometimes a difference in altitude of only a couple of feet can prevent a living thing from migrating from one zone to another every bit as effectively as a mile-high obstacle.

The Southwest, for convenience in referring to various environments and the life contained in them, is divided by naturalists into zones following a concept first proposed in the early 1890s by Dr. C. Hart Merriam, director of the Division of Ornithology and Mammalogy of the U.S. Department of Agriculture. Dr. Merriam saw the North American continent as divided into seven principal life zones: the Tropical, Lower Sonoran, Upper Sonoran, Transition, Canadian, Hudsonian and Arctic-Alpine. Although Dr. Merriam's original concept has since been

Comfortably poised on the long red legs that gave them their name, black-necked stilts congregate on a sandy bank of the Colorado just above Crystal Rapids in the Grand Canyon. Although these black-and-white wading birds have long and very flexible necks, they do not reach down to pick food off the ground. Instead, they bend their spindly legs backward at the middle and lower themselves to eat small fish and insects.

modified, his zone names are still in wide usage. The Sonoran Zones, which contain the plants and animals of the southern and central parts of the region, take their names from the state of Sonora in Mexico but apply to the United States as well. In this country only the tip of Florida falls within the southernmost, or Tropical, zone. If a man could start there and journey north at sea level he would, by the time he had gotten a trifle past Hudson Bay, have touched all seven zones and traveled about 3,000 miles. In the region of the Grand Canyon, however, one can touch all but the Tropical Zone in an airline distance of only 55 miles, and four of the seven—ranging from the cool Canadian to the hot Lower Sonoran—can be touched during a descent into the Canyon itself. In 1889 Dr. Merriam had surveyed the Grand Canyon region in an effort to discover some order in the varying climates and types of life found in its range of altitude—from 2,500 feet at the bottom of the Canyon to 12,680 feet on Humphreys Peak not far to the south. Dr. Merriam and his party observed that the zones of the region were strongly reminiscent of the broad belts of life that change with the latitudes as one journeys from Florida toward the North Pole. From his observations emerged his idea of the seven life zones, and the broad rule that in the Southwest 1,000 feet of altitude is roughly the same in its biological effects as 300 miles of latitude at sea level. Since Point Imperial, the highest point on either rim of the Grand Canyon, is about 6,300 feet above the Colorado, a descent from rim to river is the equivalent of a journey from central Canada to central coastal Mexico. The temperature on the North Rim averages 35° colder than that at the bottom of the Canyon—in February there may be as much as 12 feet of snow up on the rim while flowers bloom in the dry heat below. Snow almost never reaches the bottom: it melts and evaporates on the way down. A small amount of rain, however—about six inches a year—does get there. In the particularly moist winter of 1931-1932 the total snowfall on the North Rim amounted to 17 feet six inches. On the South Rim, about 1,500 feet lower in altitude, there was only eight feet one inch. On the Canyon floor there was none.

Other factors besides altitude and rainfall affect the life zones in the Canyon. Among them are the drainages of cool air, like unseen waterfalls, flowing over the rims and down; the upward waft of warm air; the local depth and acidity of the soil; and whether a section of the indented rim of the Canyon chances to have a southern or northern exposure. The life zones are not therefore arranged with tidy horizontality. They are irregular in shape, overlapping, interrupted. But in each life zone there are certain plants or groups of them, called "indicators," by which the zone may be recognized. The plants are joined by animals which are also zone indicators. If a naturalist sees a whiptail lizard in the same zone as a pretty scarlet mallow, he will automatically say to himself, "Lower Sonoran," just as he would say "Canadian" if he observed a quaking aspen in the company of a Colorado porcupine. Various large, wide-ranging animals are not typical of any particular zone but may be seen in several. Cougars and bobcats cover a good deal of ground, and an individual deer has been known to descend from the rim to the river and cross it in a single day.

The Lower Sonoran Zone extends from the surface of the Colorado up to about the 4,000-foot level of northern exposures and the 5,000-foot level of southern exposures within the Canyon. Like the Mexican state of Sonora, it is desert dry and hot, with summer temperatures that frequently climb above 120° in the shade. In view of its dryness, away from the banks of the river and the few streams that flow into it, there is a surprising amount of life in this lowest zone. The conditions and the competition are fierce, and each member of the community survives only because it is very tough, very unappetizing or both. A typical indicator of the Lower Sonoran is the catclaw, a straggling shrub 10 or 15 feet high, armed with sharp, curved thorns. Although not strictly confined to the zone, the smallest bat in this country, the little canyon bat, is found there; one might mistake it for a moth if it were not for its speed. There are collared lizards in the zone, the males ranging in color from yellow to bright green and the females from gray to brilliant orange. They are about a foot long with bands of light and dark stripes around their necks.

The Upper Sonoran Zone runs from about 4,000 to 6,000 feet on north-facing slopes in the Canyon, and from 5,000 to 7,000 on southern exposures. Here are found plants and animals adapted to a somewhat less severe environment, but one that is still dry and hot. The fishhook cactus is a common indicator. It looks a good deal like a furry egg covered with fishhooks, and is abundant in the surrounding desert—most of the souvenir boxes of small cacti sent home by visitors to the Southwest contain a fishhook or two. The Utah Juniper and the useful piñon pine are also Upper Sonoran, as are the gray fox and the rock squirrel.

The ponderosa pine, along with its dependent squirrels, is typical of the Transition Zone, which extends up from about 7,000 to 8,200 feet on the North Rim. Another indicator is fairly well described by its

Curved barbs shield a fishhook cactus in bloom.

Thorn-studded nodes poking out on its short branches protect a hedgehog cactus.

Entangled spines fortify a barrel cactus.

Life Besieged in the Inner Canyon

In the hostile habitat of the Grand Canyon's desert floor, survival is the definition of the good life: living things must be armed—and armored. The cacti bristle with sharp thorns to protect them against plant-loving animals. The scorpion flaunts a hard shell and a tail-end stinger that swings like a lance in the direction of danger.

When the hot sun sinks, the scorpion emerges from cover to become an efficient predator, often making kills without needing to use its poisonous sting (which can be lethal to humans in the case of the species shown at right). Added weapons are its clawlike forelimbs, with which the scorpion clutches an insect while it sucks out the victim's juices, leaving a dry husk behind. One night's catch can provide a scorpion with enough food and drink for months, even a year.

Ingenious mechanisms also sustain the Canyon's cacti, helping them conserve moisture through the worst droughts. Several species, including the barrel cactus, have pleated stems that expand rapidly as the inner pulp sops up water during the infrequent desert rains, then contract slowly as the moisture is used up. When a thirsty bird manages to tap a cactus' water supply, the plant can quickly form scar tissue to seal the wound. But the bird may fail to penetrate the plant's thorny defenses, and it may end up impaled on the cactus' spikes.

Hastily retreating from the early morning sun, a lethal scorpion scuttles across a rock.

name alone, the golden-mantled ground squirrel. Above 8,200 feet on the Kaibab Plateau, North Rim, the Canadian Zone begins and the ponderosa pine is replaced by blue spruce, white fir and Douglas fir. The Douglas fir, a cool-climate tree, is sometimes found on the South Rim, where the elevation is only 7,000 feet. Theoretically the Douglas fir has no business there; typically a Canadian Zone indicator, it ranges through the Transition Zone and even grows down in what ought to be the Upper Sonoran. This vagary occurs, however, exclusively on ledges with northern exposures just below the rim. In such places the sun seldom shines; moisture accumulates in the cool shade, making it possible for the Douglas fir to take root. The tree may grow within two or three feet of the rim but not on the rim itself. The same vagary also serves to emphasize that a map of the life zones in the Grand Canyon would show an involved pattern of zigzags, with islands of one zone often intruding into another.

Faced by a gigantic fissure that is not only a barrier to man but is also a severe obstacle to the movements of most plants and of many animals, biologists long speculated on the forms of life that might exist on the buttes that rise 5,000 or more feet from the floor of the Grand Canyon. Crowning almost perpendicular cliffs, their flat summits are like islands in space. With the case of the Kaibab squirrels in mind the biologists had some reason to dream that the buttes might also harbor variants of familiar species.

Spurred by this possibility, New York City's American Museum of Natural History announced in 1937 that it planned an expedition to the summit of Shiva Temple, a large butte near the North Rim topped by a tree-covered plateau of about 200 acres. Shiva Temple was once a promontory jutting out from the mainland of the rim, but it has been cut off by erosion for perhaps 20,000 years. It can be plainly seen from the Mather Point lookout on the South Rim, the spot from which most visitors get their first view of the Canyon.

The idea of a plateau isolated from the rest of the world for ages gave the press a field day. Newspaper feature writers recalled Arthur Conan Doyle's science-fiction novel *The Lost World* and amused themselves by suggesting that if a man managed to scale the precipitous side of the butte and peered over the rim, his head might be bitten off by a 40-foot dinosaur. The leader of the expedition, Dr. Harold Anthony, curator of mammals at the American Museum, was annoyed by such notions and by the attention they focused on him. Dr. Anthony did not ex-

An inhabitant of clefts in the Canyon walls, the cacomistle sports a luxuriant black-and-white striped tail. Despite its foxlike face and catlike body, it belongs to the raccoon family.

pect to find any nightmare creatures; he merely wished to explore Shiva Temple with an open, scientific mind to see what was up there. At most, he hoped to discover "a sidetracked descendant, somewhat differentiated, of a mammal living on the North Rim today."

Dr. Anthony's modest hopes might have been nourished by the apparently formidable problem that faced him and his party as they contemplated scaling the butte. Autogiros were available in 1937 and an approach by air was at first given serious consideration, but aerial photographs showed that the Shiva Temple summit was too densely forested to permit a landing. Reports of powerful, capricious air currents in the area indicated that it would be too dangerous to lower men by cable from a blimp or to drop them by parachute. Dr. Anthony received many suggestions from thoughtful newspaper readers as to how the plateau might be reached. One man offered to put on a football uniform and, carrying a coil of rope, jump from a low-flying plane into the treetops on the butte. After he got out of the treetops he would let the rope down the cliffside so that members of the expedition could pull themselves up. Dr. Anthony thanked him.

Ultimately it was decided that the way to reach the top of Shiva Temple was simply to climb it, and this, with the help of some experienced mountaineers from the American Geographical Society, Dr. Anthony did. The ascent was not nearly as difficult as the mountaineers expected. They went out to the butte along a narrow, dipping saddle of rock, and then climbed 1,300 feet up to the plateau. The cliffside was steplike, with alternating ledges and vertical pitches of 20 to 25 feet. The party made it to the top between daybreak and noon. The only casualty was one cut scalp caused by a small falling rock. On the first night on the butte, Dr. Anthony lit a large bonfire that could be seen from the terrace of Bright Angel Lodge 10 miles across the Canyon, and news of the successful ascent was relayed around the world.

During their several days' stay on Shiva Temple, Dr. Anthony and his companions were supplied by airdrop. Friends waiting on the rim —practical jokers—thought of using an autogiro to drop an old automobile radiator where Anthony might find it, but reconsidered the notion. However, the expedition leader did not need to find an automobile radiator to deduce that Shiva Temple had, and was still having, contact with the world below.

The relative ease with which the party had climbed to the top of the butte might have suggested that it was less of a barrier to other animals than even Dr. Anthony had believed. Then, quite soon after the exploration had begun, Dr. Anthony found the castoff antlers of several contemporary 1937-model mule deer, the tracks of a coyote and a heap of quills from a familiar species of porcupine. Bemused, he then set out several dozen small animal traps that had been hauled up the side of Shiva, placing the traps in various habitats among the rocks along the rim, under low bushes and along fallen logs in the forest. Like most other experienced naturalists who wish to catch small creatures, he used a bait made of raisins, rolled oats, cut-up bacon and peanut butter. The bait not only works well with animals but provides an occasional snack for the naturalists.

Subsequently, Dr. Anthony caught scores of wood rats, deer mice and chipmunks and from the mangled bodies of other rodents surmised that such predators as cougars and cacomistles, or ring-tailed cats, must also visit Shiva Temple. The cacomistle is not a cat at all, but closer in relationship to the raccoon. It is buff gray and about 30 inches long, but half its length consists of a first-class, admirable, bushy tail, with alternating rings of black and white. Cacomistles are beautiful. They are also intelligent, playful and sometimes even affectionate. They have been known to befriend prospectors and other lonely folk in the West; at night in the Canyon a man will sometimes see their bright, curious faces in the gloaming at the edge of the campfire.

Dr. Anthony found that the high island of Shiva had also been visited by humans, Pueblo Indians, who had climbed up to obtain the nodules of flint embedded in the Kaibab Limestone with which the butte is capped. He discovered numerous arrowheads, scrapers, drills and piles of flint chips lying where the Indians had left them—probably, according to good archeological opinion, about 1,000 years ago. It was not surprising that the Pueblos, who were cliff dwellers, should have visited Shiva, and as Dr. Anthony considered the various animals he had found on the plateau he saw at once that they too were excellent climbers. The wood rats, the deer mice and the chipmunks could very well have ascended Shiva by the route he had just followed. The mule deer were somewhat different cases; they can climb surprisingly well, but not well enough to surmount 20- to 25-foot vertical pitches in which there are only finger and toe holds.

However, there was another possible route to the summit. Anthony's mountaineers had chosen to ascend the north face of the butte where the rock surface, however steep, was fairly firm. On the south the stone had been slightly more broken down by weathering; it presented very treacherous footing for a man, but Dr. Anthony was obliged to conclude that animals did in fact use the south approach, leaping along the loose walls of rock. At the time of his ascent, in September, he concluded further that the deer climb up to the plateau in winter—he found no tracks or evidence of the animals other than the antlers, which are dropped each year in January or February.

For a time, even after he descended from Shiva Temple with the knowledge that the animals were not completely isolated, Dr. Anthony remained convinced that he had made a discovery: the small creatures he had caught in his traps seemed lighter in color than specimens taken on both rims. Possibly some significant change was slowly occurring. But after exhaustive comparison it was impossible to say that this was the case. "We may have been several thousand years too early to find tangible evidence of evolutionary changes," said Anthony, "but these will most certainly appear sooner or later, with a set-up such as that on Shiva, and I hope that they have already begun to appear."

The matter is not totally closed. Somewhere on some remote pinnacle a colony of nonclimbing animals may have been cut off. "Such a nonclimbing mammal is the pocket gopher," Dr. Anthony said, "a burrowing rodent that spends its life tunneling through the soil, and perhaps never passing more than the length of its own body from the mouth of a burrow. This animal cannot tunnel in rock, and a cliff, so far as the observations of naturalists bear testimony, should be an absolute barrier to its range." There are other nonclimbing animals in the world, other forms of life that may have been, in Anthony's words, sidetracked for 20,000 years. He died in 1970, leaving the thought for anyone with the quixotism to follow it up a wall of stone.

The North-Side Forest

Coming on the Grand Canyon from its cool, densely forested North Rim is like stepping from a dark room into the balcony of a brilliantly illuminated theater. The box seats are the points of the long fingers of land that jut out between side canyons cutting north from the Colorado gorge and extending deep into the Kaibab Plateau.

The names of most of these points reflect the excitement their discoverers, exploring the North Rim in the 1880s, felt as they emerged from the forest and looked down from the heights into the Canyon: Point Imperial, Cape Final, Cape Royal, Bright Angel Point (which overlooks the upper reaches of the famous creek of that name), Point Sublime.

Good paved roads now lead to some of these splendid overlooks, but there are more points than roads, and two can be reached only by trail. One of these trails, about 2½ miles long, goes out to Uncle Jim Point, and can be traveled on horseback. The other goes to Widforss Point, which was named, somewhat later than the others, for Gunnar Widforss, a Swedish artist who settled in the U.S. in 1921 and made a career painting the national park scenery of the West. Widforss particularly loved the Grand Canyon and spent most of the latter part of his life there until his death in 1934.

The Widforss Trail, restricted to foot travel, is a simple graded path that meanders five miles past the head of a huge side canyon called The Transept and on through the deep forest to the brow of the main Canyon. Like all good paths, the Widforss Trail appeals to several levels of interest. It offers a good day's workout for those who like to stride out and breathe deep. It presents superb and unusual views of the Canyon. It leads through one of the finest forests on earth. It is accented by displays of wild flowers and occasional sightings of birds and animals. It contains a remarkable lesson in microclimatology, with desert plants such as cactus and yucca growing in the shadow of 100-foot ponderosa pines. And it affords solitude to those who are inclined to walk or just sit undisturbed amid quiet and great beauty.

The trail's first half mile or so is a gentle ascending traverse along the north slope of a deepening valley. The trail is a little rough here because the earth is rocky and broken, and few trees have gained a foothold. But the opposite slope is

The Widforss Trail, route of the walk described on these pages, winds five miles through lofty terrain. As shown on the map below, it starts (top right) about two miles from the village of North Rim (not shown) and skirts the head of The Transept, a side canyon. It ends at Widforss Point, whose 7,650-foot elevation affords a panoramic view of nearby Oza Butte (8,065 feet) and the South Rim, nine miles away.

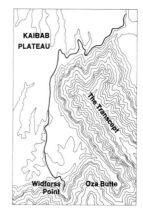

FROM THE WIDFORSS TRAIL, A VIEW OF THE TRANSEPT

covered with a mixed stand of ponderosa and white fir, with some Douglas fir and blue spruce. Ahead, the valley debouches into the northern end of The Transept.

The rock outcroppings are of the Kaibab Limestone that forms the surface of the North Rim. This layer of off-white slabby rock was laid down some 250 million years ago toward the end of the Paleozoic Era, when shallow seas covered this section of the earth. The waters must have been warm then because fossils of sponges, corals and brachiopods (commonly called lamp shells) are to be seen in the weathering stone protrusions, and even shark teeth sometimes crop up.

Prehistoric Pueblo Indians settled on the North Rim about 1,200 years ago, farming the open spaces and hunting the abundant animals of the forest. Because of its isolation the region has remained basically unchanged and an Indian hunting these woods would have seen pretty much what was observed there on a recent day in early June.

Morning—a Scurrying Lizard

Summer comes late to the North Rim because of the 8,000-foot elevation. At 8 in the morning on this June day the air was almost frosty, but it had no bite, for it was thin and dry. A hawk, probably a redtail, cruised above the dense woods of the valley slope. A short-horned lizard scurried into a patch of fallen pine needles. It would find plenty to eat among the rotting logs of the forest, many of which are infested with carpenter ants. Down below, on the floor of the little valley, a grove of quaking aspen gleamed yellow green, in sharp contrast to those back by the trail-

SHORT-HORNED LIZARD IN SEARCH OF FOOD

head, which were still almost bare of leaves. Winter retreats earlier near the great maw of the Canyon where the heated air from within it rises and flows over the rim. Near the top of the traverse lay a large lumpy rock encrusted with lichen and at its foot a wild strawberry was

SPECKLEPOD LOCOWEED

coming into leaf. The bright orange lichen may have been a thousand years old, and the strawberry plant was certainly no older than two weeks, but they both looked equally fresh and healthy.

A specklepod locoweed nestled in a small pocket. *Loco* means "crazy" in Spanish and the name refers to the way the plant affects livestock: it contains a poisonous chemical called selenium, and cattle that eat it stagger and lurch in a drunken, lunatic fashion until the effects of the chemical wear off—if it does not kill them outright.

The trail turned right and made a short excursion into the forest. In the next couple of miles it did this several times as it followed an easy gradient along the sides of the ravines. This area back from the rim

PONDEROSA, A WHITE FIR (RIGHT FOREGROUND), ASPEN (FAR RIGHT, CENTER LEFT)

is a mixed forest of white fir and Douglas fir, punctuated by aspen groves and stands of ponderosa. Fallen pine needles form a yielding carpet underfoot; there is little undergrowth and almost no grass.

Nor is there much rain during spring; as a result the aspen propagate mostly by root sprouting. They grow in groves in the sunlight away from the shadows of other trees. Aspen resembles eastern birch from a distance, but looked at closely it is denser, darker and straighter.

The bark of most trees cracks into flakes or vertical ridges as they grow and gain diameter. Not so with the chalky bark of an aspen. It stretches

STRETCH MARKS IN ASPEN BARK

ETCHINGS OF ENGRAVER BEETLES

SLENDER ELEGANCE: ASPENS IN A GROVE

QUAKING ASPEN LEAVES

during its relatively short life—a hundred years or so. A scar on a sapling, as from a detached branch, may in 30 years grow to form a lump with elongated ridges, like the lids of Buddha's eye, that stretch laterally, sometimes reaching almost clear around the trunk.

The aspen attracts a particular species of engraver beetle—one of 550 species that divide their interest among almost all the many varieties of American trees. One 10-inch aspen trunk alongside the trail displayed the beetles' intricate work. Dead bark had fallen away, exposing a web of slender grooves in the bare wood surface. Burrowing under the bark, the beetles nibble their zigzag way through the succulent phloem layer until the flow of sap is interrupted; when their tracks have girdled the tree, it dies. Such a trunk may stand long in the Kaibab forest:

if the wood escapes infection long enough to become well seasoned, it seems almost impervious to decay.

Why does aspen quake? Because the oval leaf is at an angle to the stem, and the broad, flat stem itself is quite flexible. The slightest breeze makes the leaf flutter, alternately disclosing its green upper and silvery lower surfaces.

Late Morning—Back to the Rim

Between switchbacks around the ravines the trail overlooks the head of The Transept. This rim path is probably the most dramatic part of the route. Yet those who are leery of heights need not fear it, for the trail crosses a gentle slope that curves off

easily to the cliffs below. The Transept follows the line of an ancient fault, as do many side canyons. Erosion gets a start in the crack of the fault and irresistibly eats its way down. At the bottom of The Transept a stream bed, dry much of the year, runs arrow straight three miles to join Bright Angel Creek.

The forest thins out as it approaches the edge. Here it is predominantly ponderosa, with scatterings of aspen and small white fir, looking like neat Christmas trees.

The trail leaves the rim of The Transept for the last time at about the three-mile point and descends into a shallow valley, which it fol-

HEAD OF THE TRANSEPT: OZA BUTTE AT RIGHT

lows for a few hundred yards. The valley is airy and silent, and the ponderosa are unusually tall. There is a faint fragrance of vanilla; ponderosa bark contains the same chemical compound as a vanilla plant. The bark of a mature tree is rusty orange, and as the tree grows it divides into long plates, each composed of an intricate pattern of multilayered scales, like an extraordinarily complicated jigsaw puzzle.

Early Afternoon—Seedlings and Giants

All around in this forest are trees of every size and age; seedlings barely three inches high grow at the base of 120-foot giants. Some trees are strong and healthy, others are dying from the attack of bark beetle or red rot, or have been lightning killed or storm felled. In their place clusters of young trees reach upward toward the light coming through the gaps left by the fallen pines. Most of the saplings will be crowded out; but one or two, in a hundred years or so, will grow tall enough to be struck by lightning in their turn.

Lightning sometimes simply burns off an irregular strip of bark from tip to base. In time the tree may heal, or disease may enter the wound. At other times the lightning's electric charge may travel through the sap and literally blow the tree apart in an explosion of steam. Occasionally a struck tree will catch fire. Since heavy rain usually goes with lightning, the normally flammable carpet of needles may not ignite; the trunk burns alone like a torch, leaving nothing but a fire-sculptured trunk.

Near such a stump in this part of

the forest grows a dwarf hollygrape. One species of this spiny-leaved plant, a relative of neither grape nor holly that has hollylike leaves and grapelike fruit, is a shrub; but here it creeps along the ground, its average height only a few inches. A fallen ponderosa lies next to the path where it turns and climbs from the valley floor. Not a particularly big tree, it nevertheless measures 140 feet when paced off. This small valley typifies the climax forest that exists in large sections of the Kaibab. Climax it is, but it cannot truly be called virgin after the famous and tragic game management attempt of the early 1900s.

Here in 1906 Theodore Roosevelt established a national preserve for the indigenous herd of some 4,000 splendid and vigorous mule deer. "Ecology" was a little-known word then (the 1911 edition of the *Encyclopaedia Britannica* lists it only as a subhead under plants), and the delicate balance of nature was even less understood. When mountain lions were found to be eating the mule deer, a Texan named "Uncle Jim" Owens was appointed warden to kill all such predators. During the next 12 years he killed 532 mountain lions —or so he claimed. The slaughter was joined by sportsmen and free-lancers hired by livestock companies. The official kill count by 1930 was 781 lions, 554 bobcats, 4,889 coyotes and 20 wolves.

By 1924 the Kaibab mule deer herd had grown to an estimated 100,000, with disastrous effects on the forest. Grass, shrubs and small trees were

FOREST MOSAIC: DEAD NEEDLES AND BARK

CREEPING HOLLYGRAPE IN BLOOM

A KAIBAB SQUIRREL BETWEEN MEALS

JIGSAW PATTERNS IN THE BARK OF PONDEROSA

consumed and the branches of larger trees nipped off as high as the deer could stretch. Aspen were stripped of their leaves and twigs during the next decade; each spring brought the spectacle of a half million acres of wooded park devoid of undergrowth and littered with deer carcasses.

Today hunting programs outside the park boundaries keep the deer population under some control, and the forest has almost regained its former health.

At the top of the rise the trail turns left and heads through a pure stand of ponderosa straight south toward the edge of the Grand Canyon. A woodpecker hammered away in the distance—a yellow-bellied sapsucker most likely, judging by the interrupted rhythm of his billwork.

A Kaibab squirrel could be seen high up in a tree, resting between snacks on the end of a broken branch; evidence of its efforts littered the ground under several trees next to the path. Some twig cuttings were old, perhaps left over from last year; but some, their needles green and glistening, were quite fresh.

The key to survival of this famous squirrel is the ponderosa. During midsummer and fall the squirrels busily strip the cones of scales to get at the nutritious seeds between. But now in early June, before the new seed crop ripens, they depend on the tender inner bark of the branch tips. Ponderosa pine needles are 5 to 10 inches long, growing in tufts at the ends of branches. The squirrel nipped the needle cluster off and dropped it to the ground. Then it moved back on the branch and cut off a section about four inches long, stripping it of the scaly bark. Holding the stick in its paws much as a man might eat corn on the cob, the squirrel consumed the tender underlying layer of phloem, which at this time of year is saturated by sugars produced photosynthetically by the needles. Then the squirrel dropped the woody core and went to work on another branch.

The climate is drier as the hiker nears the Canyon and this final one-and-one-half-mile section of trail is classic ponderosa forest—trim and open, with long vistas and a smooth floor of matted needles.

The ponderosa is a most adaptable tree. Found throughout the West, it mixes with the lodgepole pine in the Northwest, the Douglas fir and incense cedar in California, and the white fir in the Rockies. It will grow in any soil, even among rocks, but it flourishes on the high, dry Southwestern plateaus. It has the most efficient root system of all pines. A two-inch seedling may have a foot-long taproot. And as it rises to maturity the roots expand in all directions until they meet a competing system. Lesser trees are forced out, but the big ponderosa keep their distance from each other.

Late Afternoon—the Desert's Edge

The trail ends in a grove where the land begins to slope toward the Canyon. At this point the forest stops abruptly and the desert begins. It came as a mild shock to step so suddenly from the benign and shaded forest into that parched and dazzling world at the edge of the Canyon, the transition highlighted by a small claretcup ribbed cactus in crimson bloom.

Beyond it was a scattering of New Mexico locust, piñon pine, Utah juniper and Gambel oak clinging to the steep slope. Farther down was a tangle of mountain mahogany, waist-high and tough, with reddish-brown bark and tiny, hairy leaves.

Widforss Point itself is a rocky spine that overlooks a deep ravine on the left. Below and stretching off to the right lay Haunted Canyon, 4,000 feet deep, stark and inaccessible from above. Its west-facing wall rose in stupendous terraces to Manu and Buddha Temples. Nine miles away the South Rim stood bright in the afternoon sun, and the Coconino Plateau stretched off into the endless distance.

CLARETCUP HEDGEHOG CACTUS

END OF THE WIDFORSS TRAIL: A VIEW ACROSS THE CANYON SCREENED BY PONDEROSA PINES

3/ The Hammer and the Blade

The Canyon...is the most revealing single page of earth's history anywhere open on the face of the globe.

JOSEPH WOOD KRUTCH/ *GRAND CANYON*

Anyone who has walked along a country road after a heavy rain and noticed one of the small gullies in the earth beside it has seen the Grand Canyon of the Colorado in miniature. Both were made by erosion, one overnight and the other perhaps in two to 10 million years. There are a few other differences—the roadside gully did not have all the forces of erosion, some of which are subtle, at work on it. Essentially, however, gully and Canyon are alike. But whereas the mind readily accepts the one it has difficulty grasping the other.

One of the unsettling factors for people who live where riverbanks are usually gradual is the steepness of the Canyon walls. On the North Rim there is a place called Toroweap, where a man may walk (some men crawl) to the edge and look straight down for 3,000 feet. The region is inhabited by golden eagles; if the man is fortunate he may see one or two of them soaring far below him. Not all of the Canyon walls are so precipitous, but many of them are. This is mainly because the land drained by the Colorado is high above sea level at the river's headwaters, so that the Colorado falls 10,000 feet in its 1,400-mile course to the sea, cutting deep into the land as it goes and gushing through not one but 19 major canyons, including the Grand Canyon. On the other hand, a river that flows placidly through generally flat land—like the Mississippi—has slower and gentler cutting power. Thus the profile of the Colorado's bed is V-shaped for the greater part of its course while that of the more sluggish Mississippi is broad, shallow and saucerlike.

The steepness of the Grand Canyon and the abruptness with which one first sees it cause the viewer to doubt its age—at least two million years. In geological terms even such a span of time is reckoned as short; the Canyon is still young and growing, but visitors are inclined to search for reasons to suppose it is even younger. Thus it has been suggested by some people that the Colorado must have been until quite recently a subterranean river, and that the roof then caved in, suddenly opening up the present chasm. Other visitors take the view that the forces of earthquakes or volcanoes may have created the Canyon, that some relatively sudden violence must somehow have been involved. However, although there have indeed been moments of cataclysm in the Canyon's history, it is really, in the words of the English poet Keats, the "foster-child of silence and slow time." One national park ranger, standing near the rim to lecture on the geological history and future of the Canyon, remarked to his listeners that the Canyon was growing larger *at that moment.* Whereupon the visitors, in another of Keats' lines, "Look'd at each other with a wild surmise."

As a rule the visitors would glance along the rimrock, looking for boulders about to tip over into the abyss. Major rockfalls, however —the crash of blocks weighing many tons—are not commonly witnessed, although they are fundamental to the Canyon's growth. Not only have few people ever seen a large rockfall but not many have even heard one. In point of service at Grand Canyon, although certainly not in age, one of the senior employees of the National Park Service in the early '70s was a curator-librarian at Grand Canyon village named Louise Hinchliffe. It was her guess that in 20 years she had heard only three or four rockfalls in her part of the Canyon—and even these, she said with a smile, may have been thunderclaps or sonic booms.

The Canyon is indeed growing, as the ranger enjoyed telling visitors, but not in ways that are immediately obvious. He used to point to a patch of gray-green lichen on the limestone that forms the Canyon's edge, explaining how that insignificant and primitive plant, flat as paint and perhaps no larger in area than a dime, catches and holds its share of the 16 inches of moisture that falls on the South Rim each year. In a chemical reaction the lichen forms an organic acid that slowly decomposes the limestone. Particles of decomposed rock accumulating in a crack in the Canyon walls eventually provide enough soil to afford a roothold for the windblown seed of another larger plant. Plant succeeds plant, each sinking its roots deeper into the crack; as a plant grows and its roots expand, pressure on the surrounding rock increases. Gradually the rock weakens until—pip!—a chip breaks off and falls soundlessly into the gulf and the Canyon becomes larger by the thickness of a Bible page.

Because of the Canyon's high altitude its rims are cool at night, even in August, although during the day beneath the blazing Arizona sun the rocks become almost too hot to touch. The alternate cooling and heating, contraction and expansion, slowly helps to crumble the stone. All along the edge of the abyss grains of sand constantly trickle from crevices and sift downward.

But by far the greatest force in enlarging the Canyon is water. As rain or melted snow it seeps into cracks in the rimrock, and by freezing and thawing it widens the cracks and splits the rocks. Its most spectacular power is exerted in the floods that sweep down the gullies every year after heavy downpours or winter thaws. About once in a generation there occurs a prodigious flood that can change the Canyon's shape in a few hours more than other forces might do in many years. A single such flood can undermine cliffs, dislodge huge boulders and tear down slopes that have been undisturbed for centuries.

All of the eroded debris—from the chip dislodged by the roots of a plant to the boulder torn out by the flood—responds to further erosion and to gravity. Slowly, in a downhill journey that may take five years or as long as 500,000 years, broken rock makes its way to the brink of the Colorado and falls into the river. As it moves, it reverses its role. Once passive, now it becomes active; once pierced and pulverized by the armory of nature, now it becomes itself a blade and a hammer.

The Colorado River, as an excavator, is one of the most extraordinary devices in the natural world. Today it works under handicaps because of the dams that have been built across it and its tributaries. However, these dams are of fairly recent construction—Hoover Dam, below the Grand Canyon, was completed in 1936 and Glen Canyon Dam, above it, in 1963. There are observations and statistics that long predate them. There are accurate estimates, for example, of the amount of silt and sand the river moved every day for many years, and the average figure is 500,000 tons. For times of unfettered flood the figures are well-nigh incredible. On September 13, 1927, at a gauging station near the mouth of Bright Angel Creek in the Canyon, it was found that the Colorado was carrying 27.6 million tons of debris past that point. The measurement included only particles that were suspended in the water. There was no way of determining the amount of dissolved material or the additional tonnage of pebbles, cobblestones and boulders that rolled along the bottom, but it is thought that it may have been nearly equal. At that estimate, the river in full flood was carrying a total of about 55 million tons of material a day past the gauging station. There is really no mortal scale on which such colossal earth moving can be measured. If one attempts to think of it in conventional terms, in numbers of dump trucks, it ceases to be impressive and becomes ridiculous. To carry such a load in one 24-hour day would require a parade of more than 11 million five-ton dump trucks, passing a given point at the rate of about 125 per second.

Some of the material transported by the Colorado is blunt; it pounds. Some of it is sharp; it cuts. The effect of the river is that of a terrible and almighty rasp. It has rasped its way down through a mile of stone and in times of flood it is still rasping. The abrasive material, to be sure, comes only in small part from the Grand Canyon. It comes from the entire drainage area above the Canyon, about 150,000 square miles in five states. Until the construction of Hoover and Glen Canyon Dams the sand and silt was carried far to the west. It filled California's Imperial Valley and built a great delta in the Gulf of California. But after the dams were built this material began to settle in the reservoirs behind them. However, it is evident that there can never be enough reservoirs to contain the ceaseless accumulation—a fearful problem that the present generation bequeaths to its descendants, who will have to decide what to do with inland seas of mud behind useless dams.

It is not quite accurate to say that the Colorado River alone cut all of the Grand Canyon. The river indeed carried away almost every grain of sand that has been removed from the Canyon, but it was not the sole excavating agent. Its embayments and promontories and the buttes that rise from the Canyon floor were carved by tributary streams and by floods that sweep down the side gullies. At several times there was some spectacular volcanic action in the Canyon (radiometric dating of the lava remains puts the latest such action at about a million years ago), but aside from temporarily impounding the river behind lava dams this did almost nothing to alter the Canyon's shape. At various other times glaciers approached the Canyon but did no excavation or carving. They doubtless had another effect, however. When the ice melted, the floods that swept down the river must have been appalling, and the rasping far more severe than it has ever been since.

Geological faults—fractures in the layers of the earth's crust—also

had much to do with shaping the Canyon. There are at least a dozen transverse faults through it, the most famous being the Bright Angel, which is responsible for a secondary canyon that runs from rim to rim, making possible a good cross-Canyon trail. And even more than such faults, other kinds of earth movements most likely have played fundamental roles in the Canyon's geological history.

There could have been no Grand Canyon at all if an uplift of the region had not occurred many millions of years ago to create the plateau through which the Colorado cuts. The plateau, called the Kaibab north of the Canyon and the Coconino south of it, is not as flat as the word implies. Its profile is often described as dome-shaped, although that suggests too high a curve; blister-shaped is more accurate. In any case, the Canyon runs through the blister, somewhat south of center. This accounts for the fact that the North Rim is on the average 1,200 feet higher than the South. Because the ground slopes down toward the North Rim, precipitation there drains into the Canyon, while water falling on the South Rim drains away from it. The north side therefore has had more flooding over its rims, which have retreated because they have suffered more erosion. Thus the bed of the Colorado River is closer to the south side of the Canyon.

To understand the forces that raised the plateau, one must abandon any idea of the solidity and endurance of hills, mountains and rocks. Do not trust rocks. A rock resting on the rim of the Grand Canyon may give an impression of strength and permanence, but as soon as a man turns his back the rock will resume disintegrating and sneaking off to California. And it is not only that particular rock that is unreliable. Every rock everywhere is growing smaller or larger, rising up or sinking down, or creeping around the planet in a scandalous manner.

Layers of rocks that are beneath the sea are increasing in thickness because of sedimentation. Rocks above the sea are diminishing because of erosion. (The etymology of the word is worth noting. It is the noun form of "erode," which derives from the Latin verb *rodere*, "to gnaw," as does the word rodent.) There is a respected geophysical theory that entire continents are, or have been, drifting apart as a result of sea-floor spreading. A point often made to illustrate the theory is that Africa and South America on a world map resemble adjacent pieces of a jigsaw puzzle that have become separated.

Everyone is aware of the movement of rocks that is caused by volcanic action. It occurs all the time. In 1943 a Mexican farmer working

in his field plowed up a wisp of smoke. A volcano called Paricutín sprouted in the furrow and now the poor man's field is buried several hundred feet beneath a cinder cone. Pressures within the earth can also move immense masses of rocks very quietly and inconspicuously, with not the slightest smoke or sound. For example, the Pacific coast in the Los Angeles area is known to be subsiding at the rate of almost five feet every hundred years.

If one bears in mind the enormousness of geological time and the impermanence or movement of rocks, the transformation of formerly low-lying land into an 8,000-foot-high plateau is easier to grasp. During a period geologists call the Laramide Revolution, between 30 and 60 million years ago, there was a great deal of rising among the rocks of the West—the Rocky Mountains were formed and so, too, was the blisterlike plateau through which the Grand Canyon has been cut. At that time the ancestral Colorado River was prevented by the plateau from flowing west, as it now does. Instead it flowed south and east, possibly having an outlet in the Gulf of Mexico. On the western side of the blister there was another, separate drainage system called the Hualapai, which flowed toward California. The two systems remained separate for millions of years, although the Hualapai was slowly gnawing its way eastward into the plateau by a process called headward erosion. As rain and melted snow drained off the top of the plateau, they formed channels that also extended up and into the slope.

About 12 million years ago, it is thought, there occurred still more uplifting of the rocks of the Southwest. At that time, if the ancestral Colorado ever had an outlet in the Gulf of Mexico, it was blocked. The river then formed a huge lake in northeastern Arizona and continued to flow into it. Meanwhile the Hualapai drainage system went on gnawing eastward until at last it cut its way completely across the plateau and captured the ancestral Colorado in a maneuver geologists call stream piracy. All of the water then began to flow west and the modern river was born. Its date of birth was, more or less, 10 million years ago. The huge lake dried up and vanished, although its sediments remain to indicate where it once existed.

Some geologists believe that at the time of the linking of the two drainage systems the plateau was much lower than it is today. It continued to rise but apparently it never rose fast enough to impede the flow of the Colorado, and as the river continued to cut downward the Canyon walls rose higher and higher. An old analogy is to a cake and a knife: instead of the knife pressing down against the cake, the cake

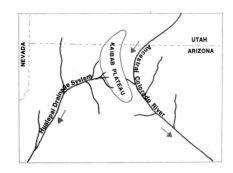

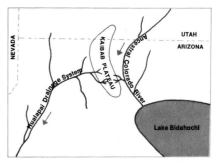

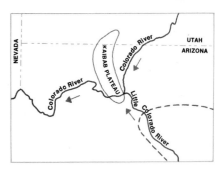

The Colorado River, architect of the Grand Canyon, evolved from two ancient river systems, according to a theory traced in these diagrams. About 35 million years ago (top), the Kaibab Plateau separated the Hualapai and the ancestral Colorado Rivers. Some 23 million years later (center), the Colorado formed Lake Bidahochi, while the Hualapai eroded its way eastward. Eventually, the Hualapai broke through the plateau (bottom), diverting the Colorado into its channel.

presses up against the knife. Whatever the case, similar risings may be found in many parts of this tormented planet, but in very few places is there the combination of rising ground and roaring river that has produced the Grand Canyon. Theodore Roosevelt was not far wrong when in advocating the preservation of its unspoiled wilderness he described it as "a natural wonder which, so far as I know, is in kind absolutely unparalleled throughout the rest of the world."

While the plateau was rising, stresses in its various layers became too great, causing the rock to slip farther along ancient fault lines. Perhaps the ground is still rising. The possibility of slippage and earthquakes still exists, but no one worries much about it. Of far greater interest are the layers of rock themselves and what they reveal of the history of the earth.

The commonly used rounded figure of 10 million years refers only to the length of time that has elapsed since the river began to cut the Canyon. The rocks that were cut are much older, almost unbelievably older. From various overlooks on the Canyon rim one can see into its deepest part, a narrow, V-shaped slot called Granite Gorge, where the river flows a mile deep in stone. The walls of the gorge are formed mainly of Vishnu Schist, a type of rock that is very hard and very dark, almost black. Although the figure of 10 million may have prepared a man to think in large terms, it cannot have prepared him for this: the rock is two billion years old, among the most ancient rock exposed anywhere on the face of the earth.

While geologists do not all agree as to exactly how the Colorado River came to be where it is, there is less uncertainty regarding these rocks, or regarding most of the other rock layers in the Canyon. They are plainly legible, with their message written in the form of crystals, granules, slants, bends, radioactivity, textures, colors and fossils. And here again, although a man may be prepared to accept the idea that rocks move, he cannot be prepared for this: the black rocks of Granite Gorge are all that remain—the roots—of mountains that may once have towered as high as the Rockies. Some of the black rocks were sedimentary in origin, others volcanic, but now they have been so changed, metamorphosed, by heat and pressure that it requires a trained eye to distinguish which was originally sedimentary and which volcanic. Two billion years ago movements of the earth's crust warped and squeezed the rocks into mountains; then, during countless millions of years of erosion, the mountains were worn down until only a low, flat plain remained. This in turn was covered by the waters of an ancient lake or sea in which there accumulated layer upon layer of sediments, to which geologists have given such names as Bass Limestone, Hakatai Shale and Shinumo Quartzite.

The layers of sedimentary stone piled up until they were at least two miles thick above the old mountain roots. Colored in vermilion and brown and purple, these layers contain the oldest fossils that have yet been found in the Canyon: the remains of primitive plants and invertebrates. When the layers of stone became deeper than two miles, perhaps 12,000 feet, they were transformed into new mountain ranges, quite different in character from the old. These were mountains made when weak areas in the flat sedimentary deposits broke and tilted upward. After more millions of years of ceaseless erosion, they too were leveled. In some places they were entirely swept away, again exposing the black root plain on which they had risen; elsewhere slanting wedges remained to bear witness to what had taken place. Once more the waters advanced and these wedges became islands jutting above the surface of a sea until they also vanished beneath layers of sediment thousands of feet thick.

Through ages so vast that they boggle the mind the land rose and fell, rose and fell, sometimes above and sometimes beneath the sea, building and eroding, a process that continues to this instant. As more layers were created they remained generally flat and parallel—limestone, sandstone and shale in various sequences: Tapeats Sandstone, Bright Angel Shale, Redwall Limestone, Supai Sandstone. The rimrock today is Kaibab Limestone. In the ascending formations are found fossils of ascending forms of life—trilobites (primitive crablike animals), fish, the tracks of amphibians and reptiles—and in the limestone rimrock there are fossil corals, suggesting that the environment of the region was once tropical or subtropical. To walk from the bottom of the Canyon to the top is almost literally to walk through time. In the depths a man can sense, in a phrase of Herman Melville's, "God's foot upon the treadle of the loom," and on the heights he can see, for better or worse, the creature man.

It is a walk that will be taken in pages to come, from one rim of the Canyon to the other, among the colors and the pinnacles and the cliffs. It is not a walk that will be taken with any references to religion, which abound in the literature of the Canyon. A man's faith or lack of it need not be thrust upon anyone else. There is, however, a particular hymn that may perhaps be quoted at the end of a chapter about the geology of the Canyon without giving offense to anyone. It chances to be a Christian hymn but it is based upon a prayer of Moses, the 90th Psalm. It is "Our God, Our Help in Ages Past," written by the 18th Century English clergyman and poet Isaac Watts. The Reverend Mr. Watts had probably never heard of the Grand Canyon, and certainly did not have the Canyon in mind when he wrote his hymn. Its majestic melody is known to everyone who has been within earshot of a church on a Sunday morning, but not many people except choristers are really familiar with its last four stanzas. It is likely, if a man lives in the English-speaking world, that he will hear this hymn sung, somewhere, at least once more before he dies. Then, if he has ever known them, he may think of the Canyon and the river.

Before the hills in order stood, or earth received her frame,
From everlasting Thou art God, to endless years the same.

A thousand ages in Thy sight are like an evening gone;
Short as the watch that ends the night before the rising sun.

Time, like an ever-rolling stream, bears all its sons away;
They fly forgotten, as a dream dies at the opening day.

Our God, our Help in ages past, our Hope for years to come,
Be Thou our Guard while troubles last, and our eternal home.

Forces That Made the Canyon Grand

Standing on the rim of the Grand Canyon, gazing across this giant wound in the earth's surface, a visitor might assume that the Canyon had been caused by some ancient convulsion. In fact, the events that produced the Canyon, far from being sudden and cataclysmic, simply add up to the slow and orderly process of erosion.

Many millions of years ago the Colorado Plateau in the Grand Canyon area contained 10,000 more feet of rock than it does today, and was relatively level. The additional material consisted of some 14 layered formations of rock. In the Grand Canyon region these layers were largely worn away over the course of millions of years, exposing the Canyon's present top layer of Kaibab Limestone, a rock formation 250 million years old.

Approximately 65 million years ago, the plateau's flat surface in the Grand Canyon area bulged upward from internal pressure; geologists refer to this bulging action as upwarping; it was followed by a general elevation of the whole Colorado Plateau, a process that is still going on. As the plateau gradually rose, shallow rivers that meandered across it began to run more swiftly and cut more definite courses. One of these rivers, located east of the upwarp, was the ancestor of the Colorado. Another river system called the Hualapai, flowing west of the upwarp, extended itself eastward by cutting back into the upwarp; it eventually connected with the ancient Colorado and captured its waters. The new river then began to carve out the 277-mile-long trench that eventually became the Grand Canyon. Geologists estimate that this initial cutting action began no earlier than 10 million years ago.

Since then, the canyon-forming has been cumulative. To the corrosive force of the river itself, dropping through the Canyon walls on an average gradient of 7.8 feet per mile—a rate 25 times that of the lower Mississippi—have been added other factors. Heat and cold, rain and snow, along with the varying resistance of the rocks, increase the opportunities for erosion. The Canyon walls crumble; the river acquires a cutting tool, tons of debris; rainfall running off the high plateau creates feeder streams that carve side canyons. Pushing slowly backward into the plateau, the side canyons expose new rocks and the pattern of erosion continues.

The continuity of the original plateau, cleft by the channel of the Colorado River, is still apparent in the opposing walls of the North and South Rims (at a point about 12 miles into the Canyon). Here, only four of the Canyon's 20 basic layers of rock have been exposed by the cutting action of the river.

The Slow Destruction of Ancient Stone

An outcropping of Kaibab Limestone (left) succumbs inexorably to the elements and the biological action of plants, a process less dramatic than the cutting action of the river but no less important to the shaping of the Canyon. Beaten by wind and rain, baked by heat, chilled by ice and snow, penetrated by rivulets of water that freeze and thaw, the rocks are gradually cracked and flaked away. Shallow pockets of rocky soil nurture windblown seeds of grass and piñon pine whose expanding roots contribute to the degradation, and even the seemingly gentle lichens generate acids that relentlessly eat into the surface of the hardest rocks.

Triggered by the combined forces of erosion, a rockfall in Marble Canyon (right) has deposited a whole section of Canyon wall in the river—fresh grist for the water's grinding action. When such a fall occurs the face of the cliff may be suddenly and dramatically altered. This fall, from a point high on the Canyon rim, exposed a broad band of the original cream color of the Kaibab Limestone, in striking contrast to the surrounding weathered rock. Meanwhile, at the rim the rockfall has bitten another few feet from the plateau.

Patterns of Erosion:
Time and Rock

*The Canyon at Nankoweap Rapids
(left) exposes eight layers of rock, each
of which has its own pattern of erosion.
The hard rocks form sheer cliffs,
the soft rocks crumble into slopes and
benches. The typical stair-step
formation of the Canyon walls arises
partly from this variation in hardness,
partly from the fact that higher
portions of the walls have been
exposed longer and have had more
time to erode than those lower down.*

*Rocks dislodged by erosion from the
Canyon wall choke the river at Crystal
Rapids (right). Tumbling along the
bottom, scouring and smoothing each
other as they go, they provide the
river's cutting power and help deepen
its channel. In years past, before a dam
completed in 1963 upstream at Glen
Canyon checked the river's flow, the
Colorado surged along at speeds and
in volumes great enough to carry an
average of 500,000 tons of rocky debris
and sediment through the Grand Canyon
each day. Under flood conditions this
daily tonnage rose to 27 million—and
the force of the current was sufficient
to carry along six-foot boulders.*

KAIBAB LIMESTONE

TOROWEAP LIMESTONE

COCONINO SANDSTONE

HERMIT SHALE

SUPAI SANDSTONE

REDWALL LIMESTONE

MUAV LIMESTONE

BRIGHT ANGEL SHALE

TAPEATS SANDSTONE

GRAND CANYON SERIES

ZOROASTER GRANITE

BRAHMA AND VISHNU SCHIST

A Layered Look Upward through Time

At its deepest point, along the stretch known as Granite Gorge, the Canyon slices about a mile into the earth's crust and two billion years into its past. It has been called the world's oldest and largest history book—and yet its striated pages tell only part of the story. Geologists divide the earth's history into four great chronological eras, but the Canyon walls represent only the earliest two, the Precambrian and the Paleozoic (chart at far right); all the rocky evidence of the two most recent eras, the Mesozoic and Cenozoic, has been worn away by erosion. The rocks that remain, however, record some spectacular geological events. The oldest of the Canyon's rocks, the schists at the bottom of the gorge, are relics of a time when the earth's roiling center disturbed its surface—they are rocks turned on end by internal pressure, charged chemically by heat, then infiltrated by molten streams of mineral matter. Above them, the seven tilted layers of rock called the Grand Canyon Series were set aslant by an uplift of vast dimensions along fault lines in the earth's crust.The Canyon's uppermost layers of sandstone, limestone and shale reflect the imprint of a long procession of seas, deserts and riverine flood plains, each with its own sediment, distinct in composition and color from those below and above.

A GRAND CANYON GEOLOGICAL TIMETABLE			
ROCK FORMATION	APPROXIMATE AGE IN MILLIONS OF YEARS	PERIOD	ERA
KAIBAB LIMESTONE	250	PERMIAN	PALEOZOIC
TOROWEAP LIMESTONE	255		
COCONINO SANDSTONE	260		
HERMIT SHALE	265		
SUPAI SANDSTONE	285	PENNSYLVANIAN	
REDWALL LIMESTONE	335	MISSISSIPPIAN	
TEMPLE BUTTE LIMESTONE*	355	DEVONIAN	
MUAV LIMESTONE	515	CAMBRIAN	
BRIGHT ANGEL SHALE	530		
TAPEATS SANDSTONE	545		
GRAND CANYON SERIES	1,200		PRECAMBRIAN
ZOROASTER GRANITE	1,700		
BRAHMA AND VISHNU SCHIST	2,000		

* Not visible in picture

Listed above is the succession of layers of Grand Canyon rock with their approximate ages and the geologic eras and periods in which they were formed. The orderly progression of rock formation from the Precambrian Era through the entire span of the Paleozoic Era is interrupted by many aberrations. The most obvious of these aberrations once included 12,000 feet of rock that lay above the Vishnu Schist and was largely removed by erosion before the Tapeats Sandstone was laid down. The eroded materials—their remnants are still visible in the Grand Canyon Series—are known to geologists as The Great Unconformity.

A Canyon-building Complex of Tributaries

Intersecting the rims of the Canyon, both visible in the photograph, hundreds of tributary streams cut their own canyons. Rasping away at the rock in emulation of the great river they feed, the tributaries are largely fed by the runoff from torrential rains and melting snow, and they flow intermittently. But their force, funneled down cracks and depressions (some created by the fault lines of the original plateau), is sufficient to carve out a pattern of steep-sided gorges. Those on the North Rim, seen at left in the photograph, are more numerous. They also extend much farther back into the plateau—well beyond the area pictured. These special characteristics of the North Rim's side canyons are largely a matter of relative rainfall and drainage. The North Rim's annual rainfall averages 25 inches and all of it funnels down the southward-sloping plateau into the Canyon; the rainfall of the South Rim totals only 16 inches a year, but much of it, also flowing southward, drains away from the Canyon. The North Rim is so deeply excavated by side canyons that in certain sections its pattern resembles a giant-toothed comb. The side canyons of the South Rim merely serrate it in gentle scallops. Although many of the side canyons intersecting both rims are too minor to have received names, a few—such as Havasu and Kanab Canyons—are many miles long, with perennially flowing streams and tributary canyon systems of their own.

Shrinking Monuments to a Vanished Rim

Its once substantial connection to the North Rim reduced to a narrow rocky spur between two side canyons, a promontory with the Wagnerian name of Wotan's Throne (left), illustrates the effects of eons of frost, plant growth and runoff from cloudbursts, thundershowers and snowmelt. The tendency of water running down an incline to cut the slope backward—geologists call it headward erosion—is gradually pushing the side canyons deeper into the plateau and at the same time narrowing the divisions between adjacent side canyons. The end of this process, the destruction of the connecting spur, isolates a section of rim and forms free-standing buttes like Vishnu Temple (right).

Silhouetted against the morning sun, 7,529-foot-high Vishnu Temple was once part of the rim. Isolated first by headward erosion, then attacked on all sides by the forces of weathering, Vishnu gradually shrank to its present shape and acquired its distinctive peaked top. Vishnu was named by an explorer who thought such peaks looked like Oriental temples and so labeled them; Vishnu is a Hindu god.

A Spectacle Destined for Oblivion

Of the dozens of so-called temples that dot the Canyon's inner landscape, three are visible in the photograph at right. Each has reached a different stage in the long process of decay that began even before they were separated from the rim. Much of Shiva's 7,618-foot summit, at the extreme left, has weathered away to Coconino Sandstone, though it still retains traces of the Kaibab Limestone rim, and the rim's underlying layer of Toroweap Limestone. Both 7,012-foot Isis in the center and 6,637-foot Osiris, on the far right, are capped entirely in Coconino Sandstone. But while Isis' top is still relatively broad and flat, Osiris' Coconino cap has largely worn away, and only a pinnacle is left. In less than a million years, the cap will be gone, and when it goes the two lower layers of comparatively soft Hermit Shale and Supai Sandstone will break down faster than the overlying sandstone and limestone strata. Thereafter, Osiris should have a respite, for the next layer, of Redwall Limestone, is almost as resistant to the forces of erosion as Osiris' one-time Kaibab Limestone cap.

4/ The Climb Down

*The discoveries to be made within this Canyon
are worth the efforts required to get down....Within those
red walls exist innumerable little worlds,
surprising worlds, and hundreds of hidden paradises....*

ANN AND MYRON SUTTON/ *THE WILDERNESS WORLD OF THE GRAND CANYON*

There are people of a certain spirit who, having looked at the Grand
Canyon from the rim, must descend into it. And once they have done
so they never forget the experience. Sometimes they return as much as
20 or even 40 years later, perhaps with their children or grandchildren,
to make the descent again. Not long ago two young Marines on leave
were hiking into the Canyon on the Bright Angel Trail when they saw
to their shock what appeared to be the body of an old lady wedged in
some rocks. It was indeed an old lady, but when the Marines reached
her they found that she was alive and, under the circumstances, well.
On the preceding afternoon she had been walking down the trail alone,
had stumbled and fallen off it and had spent the night in the rocks. The
Marines carried her down to the nearest ranger station, at Indian Gardens, where it turned out that her injuries were only cuts, bruises and a
knock on the head. She was 76 years old.

"I last saw Indian Gardens 30 years ago," she said to the ranger,
"and I just thought I'd come down and look at it again." In a short time
she began to make jokes about her fall and said that she felt well enough
to hike back out of the Canyon. The ranger, lost in admiration for her,
would not permit the lady to chance this but arranged for her to be
taken out by helicopter.

Of the people who make the descent on muleback, a good many actually remember the names of their mules—Ace, Pistol, Napoleon—for the rest of their lives. It sometimes happens that the mule guides are confronted by elderly citizens who ask, "Is Napoleon still here? I want to ride him again."

Mules are long-lived, occasionally reaching 25 to 30 years, and conceivably Napoleon may still be present although the likelihood is that he is dead or in retirement. (Superannuated Grand Canyon mules are not turned into dog meat. When they become too old to cope with the trails the man in charge of them, whose title is Chief of Transportation, sells them at a livestock auction. Almost always among the dog-meat buyers he is able to spot someone who wants to purchase the animal as a child's pet. A deal is made and the fortunate mule spends the rest of its days in comfort.) In any case, if Napoleon is gone the mule guides may still say, "Why, sure—there he is," and point to a creature named Betsy. The rider is delighted.

The steady, rocking motion of the mules is described musically in the section of Ferde Grofé's *Grand Canyon Suite* called "On the Trail." The concessionaire who conducts the trips furnishes customers with a leaflet cautioning them in various languages not to undertake the journey "If you have fear of height . . . *Si vous craignez l'altitude . . . Sollten Sie unter Höhenangst . . . Si usted tiene miedo a las alturas. . . .*" The only restrictions are that the riders be at least 12 years old, in apparent good health, and weigh not more than 200 pounds fully clothed. However there are problems. Although there are already too many mules in the park, wearing out trails that cost $1,000 per mile per year to maintain, mule trips are extremely popular and reservations for them must be made months in advance. And of course riders accompanying mule trains have no control over pace or pause, but must maintain their places in the train and stop only when it does. It is better, if one has the time and is in good health, to walk.

Those who prefer to make it on their own find that hiking in the Canyon is physically the opposite of mountain climbing. A man starts downhill when he is fresh and goes uphill, if he returns the same day, when he is tired. He also enters the thinner air of the high rims at the end of his journey, when his heart and lungs are working hard. There are at least 19 trails down into the Canyon, almost all of them originally made by deer, bighorn sheep, Indians and prospectors. Almost all have been abandoned and today, because of washouts and rockslides, several of them are difficult and dangerous. Only two, the Bright Angel and the Kaibab, are maintained by the National Park Service. The Bright Angel Trail begins near Grand Canyon village and winds 7.8 miles to reach the river 4,500 feet below—not far from Phantom Ranch (which is on the north bank of the Colorado). The trail is on the average five feet wide, and mules have the right of way. If a hiker encounters a mule train he stands on the outside of the trail, trying not to teeter backward, until the train has passed. At Indian Gardens the hiker may see one of the smallest bulldozers in all creation, about the size of an office desk. The bulldozer, which is used to keep the campground level, was driven down the trail a few years ago by some brave men. The machine is four feet eight inches wide and thus had a clearance of two inches on each side of the five-foot trail. The drivers, who took turns, had strong ropes tied around their bodies, and the ends were held by men walking behind. The idea was that if the bulldozer had gone over a cliff these men might perhaps have saved the fellow at the controls.

The other maintained trail, the Kaibab, begins near Yaki Point, about 4.5 miles east of Grand Canyon village. Constructed between 1924 and 1928 with the aid of jackhammers and many tons of dynamite, it is the only trail that crosses the Canyon. From the South Rim it descends 4,800 feet in 7.1 miles, crosses the suspension bridge over the Colorado, and then follows Bright Angel Canyon for 13.5 miles up to the North Rim, ending near Grand Canyon Lodge at an elevation of 8,200 feet. In its entire 20.6-mile length from rim to rim there is only one quarter of a mile that is not reached by the sun's rays. Thus the trail is generally free of snow, and along its south section it makes use of a series of ridges for natural drainage. This section is, however, steep and is recommended "only for descent and only by the sturdiest of hikers."

Still, the Kaibab is just a test for those who would venture onto any of the abandoned trails in the Canyon. Before they do so, the Park Service requires that they serve an apprenticeship on the Kaibab or the Bright Angel. They must also register at a ranger station, state their proposed route and expected time of return, and submit to an inspection of their equipment. The ranger is also empowered to refuse hiking permission to people who do not impress him as being physically able to undertake such a journey.

Inspection of equipment such as canteens is a reasonable precaution: in the dry heat of the inner Canyon as much as two gallons—16 pounds—of water may be evaporated from a man's body in a day. According to one ranger, "A canteen with less than one-gallon capacity is only a toy." A gallon is the absolute minimum required for a hike from the river up to the rim. It is lack of water, more than any other cause, that accounts for casualties in the Canyon. A single example may suffice to make the point. In the late 1950s a 32-year-old priest who had apparently climbed down one of the abandoned trails—the Tanner—in his youth, took two teen-aged boys on a vacation in the West. They started down the trail without registration or inspection, carrying only one bottle of water and a can of beans among them. They lost their way and evidently the priest became irrational. He suggested that all three remove their shoes and throw them over an 80-foot cliff—which was done. In trying to descend the cliff the priest lost his footing, fell and was killed. The boys managed to go around the cliff and down, but one of them died of thirst on the way to the river. The survivor succeeded in reaching the Colorado, where he lived for a week before he was seen by a helicopter pilot and lifted out.

Although there are several tales of dreadful falls down the cliffs of the Canyon, the truth is that they do not occur very often. Most people have a decent respect for heights. John Muir, the great naturalist and founder of the Sierra Club, had bad dreams about them. Major John Wesley Powell, a man of unquestioned courage, once wrote: "We walk out to the brink of the canyon, and look down to the water below. I can do this now, but it has taken several years of mountain climbing to cool my nerves, so that I can sit, with my feet over the edge, and calmly look down a precipice 2,000 feet. And yet I cannot look on and see another do the same. I must either bid him come away, or turn my head."

When injuries do occur in the Canyon they are most likely to be broken bones or bad sprains incurred when hikers step carelessly on loose rocks. The most experienced of all Canyon hikers is Dr. Harvey Butchart, a professor of mathematics at Northern Arizona University, who in the past 25 years has spent more than 750 climbing days there and covered about 16,000 miles. In all of his travels in the Canyon he has suffered a really serious injury only once, when he made "an inconsequential little jump," landed awkwardly, and broke a bone in his heel. He had to be helicoptered out.

Dr. Butchart's routes, carefully drawn on a map of the Canyon in his study, resemble an enormous fingerprint. He has made his way across some incredibly difficult terrain and has frequently crossed quiet pools in the Colorado on his inflated air mattress. (The practice is strongly condemned by Park Service men, who point out that one of Dr. Butchart's companions was drowned while attempting it.)

Several of the abandoned trails lead to old mining claims—there were once 83 of them in the Canyon, from which asbestos, copper, silver, platinum, lead and bat guano were extracted. Metallic ores were not profitable to remove because they had to be transported by burros or mules, which could carry only 100 or 175 pounds respectively. Near the western end of the Canyon there is an enormous cave whose floor is several feet deep in bat guano, dropped over thousands of years. In the 1950s the value of the guano as nitrate fertilizer was estimated at 12.5 million dollars. A two-mile tramway including one 8,100-foot span, one of the longest in the world, was built to carry the guano out. However, cheaper sources of nitrate were soon developed and the operation came to an end. The tramway remained until 1960, when a military airplane flew into its steel cable at a terrific speed. Astonishingly, the plane was only dented and was brought to a safe landing. Thereafter the tramway cables were cut down. For some time the owners of the guano deposit employed a reclusive Englishman to live near the cave and guard it from trespassers. The Englishman, in the manner of his breed, was fond of pets, but the only pets he could keep in that dry, grim location were scorpions and lizards. He used to feed the former to the latter.

The remains of mining camps in the Canyon are occasionally of interest to certain hikers. Some of the trash dumps, preserved for fourscore years in the dry atmosphere, yield interesting scraps of paper, tools and the like. The mine shafts, however, are dangerous, full of foul air and likely to collapse. Other abandoned trails in the western part of the Canyon sometimes afford hikers a glimpse of a bighorn sheep or a wild burro. The burros, which were released years ago by miners who quit their claims and left the Canyon, are native not to North America but to North African countries. They are able to subsist on almost any sort of vegetation, and consequently they reduce the forage of the bighorn sheep, which *are* native. It is possible that the wild burros allowed to multiply unchecked could cause the extinction by starvation of the bighorns in the Canyon. Therefore the Park Service in its good and certainly correct judgment has caused rangers and professional hunters to shoot the burros.

The abandoned Canyon trails are fascinating and have tremendous appeal for knowledgeable and vigorous climbers. However, for those who are not notably athletic but still in decent physical condition a hike across the Canyon from rim to rim on the maintained trails is one of the most spectacular in the world. The walk is usually begun on the North—it is higher than the South Rim, farther removed from towns and public transportation, and not as convenient a place in which to emerge after three or four days on the trail.

The approach to the North Rim is made through high meadows and forests of pine, spruce and fir. Among the evergreens are groves of aspen, their leaves quaking in the slightest breeze. Botanists explain the trembling by pointing to the long, slender, flattened stems of the leaves, which allow free motion, but among certain Christian sects, particularly in French Canada, there is a more colorful opinion. They believe that the Cross of the Crucifixion was made of aspen wood and that the tree trembles eternally in repentance. The North Rim aspens are well known to Western photographers and painters, who journey for miles in the fall to make pictures of their golden-yellow leaves.

A hiker who descends the north Kaibab Trail, crosses the river near Phantom Ranch and ascends the Bright Angel Trail will cover about 23 miles. It is possible for an athlete to do this in one day—a runner in top condition, indeed, using only the Kaibab Trail, once set a rim-to-rim record of three hours 56 minutes. (It is also possible for a runner in top condition to pass by all the paintings in the Grand Gallery of the Louvre in about 28 seconds.) For good sturdy hikers, crossing the Canyon in two days, breaking the trip at Phantom Ranch, is easy enough. However, four days is a more reasonable length of time. It allows for side trips, photography and contemplation. Campgrounds are spaced so that the downhill walk may be broken into two segments of about seven miles each, and the uphill into segments of five, and four and a half miles. If help must be summoned by emergency telephone, a mule guide will come down the trail leading a spare mount. This service, depending on where the hiker has quit, costs from $25 to $50, cash in advance. Exhausted hikers are called "drag-outs" and are not highly admired by the Chief of Transportation, a leathery man named Jay Goza. "It used to be," he says, "that after we had carried a drag-out up to the rim, he'd tell us he didn't have any money. Now we get the money *first*. If the drag-out says he doesn't have any, we just let him lie there, turn the mules around and start back up the trail. Pretty quick by some kind of miracle the money drops into his pocket out of the sky and he yells for us to come back." The Chief of Transportation, reflecting on a recent season, could not recall having dragged out anyone older than 40, although as noted earlier many people far older than that make the hike. "The drag-outs were mostly between 18 and 25," he said, shaking his head, "and mostly male. How do you like that?"

The descent from the North Rim begins fairly steeply as the trail cuts down through the horizontal layers of rock that parallel the contours of the Canyon wall. The upper layers, 500 to 700 feet thick, are first the Kaibab and then the Toroweap formations, both limestones and both cream-colored. They were laid down 250 and 255 million years ago at the bottom of a warm sea and contain many fossils of sponges, corals, snails and clams. The limestones are hard, weathering into cliffs rather than breaking down into slopes. Below them is one of the Canyon's most prominent formations, the Coconino Sandstone, a wide white band of cemented quartz grains. The Coconino too is hard and is also a cliff but was formed at a time when the region was not a sea but a desert. The entire formation of the Coconino Sandstone is flat and parallel with the two others, but *within* the formation there are beds of rock that slant in various directions. These represent the hardened remains of ancient sand dunes, and differences in the angles at which they slant indicate how the prevailing winds changed direction—as they did about 260 million years ago.

As a hiker makes his way down past the Coconino Sandstone he encounters an interbedded mixture of formations, the Hermit Shale and the Supai Sandstone, from 500 to 1,300 feet thick, generally red in color, containing layers of sandstones, shales and siltstones. Shale, which is hardened mud, is the weakest of the formations and thus the most easily eroded. The alternation of rock layers accounts for the characteristic symmetrical shapes within the Canyon. Profiles called "triple S"—scarp, shelf, slope—have been developed because the hard sandstones and limestones erode as scarps or cliffs, while the softer shales between them erode as slopes and shelves. Some of the great cliffs are maintained in nearly vertical condition by undermining: when the shale beneath them is eaten away, straight-sided blocks break off the sandstone or limestone cliffs as though chopped with a cleaver.

Examples of triple-S erosion can be seen everywhere in the Canyon walls and in the step-sided mesas and buttes that rise like truncated pyramids from the floor. On their tops there are protective layers of hard cap rock such as Coconino Sandstone; beneath the cap rock the scarps, shelves and slopes of these formations flare out and down symmetrically, falling into a broad base. The triple-S profiles suggest to some observers the shapes of Oriental pagodas or temples such as Angkor Wat in Cambodia, and it is from this circumstance that many of the place names in the Canyon derive. When Major John Wesley Powell made his explorations he bestowed names left and right and often honored his friends. The Howlands, Hawkins and Dunn Buttes in the Canyon are named for his boatmen. Powell also had a fine flair for the descriptive—Dirty Devil, Bright Angel, Flaming Gorge, Desolation Canyon, Lava Falls and the like.

Immediately in Powell's footsteps came a protégé of his, Clarence Dutton of the U.S. Geological Survey, an excellent geologist and writer, who was interested in architecture and Eastern religions. It was Dutton who produced the first important geological book—and still one of the finest—on the area, *The Tertiary History of the Grand Cañon District*, published in 1882. In his book Dutton gave the Canyon's features such names as Vishnu Temple, Brahma Temple and Hindu Amphitheater. Following Dutton's example other students of the Canyon ventured into Nordic and Mediterranean religion and mythology, so that hikers in various parts of the Canyon today are confronted with Wotan's Throne, Siegfried Pyre, Venus Temple, Apollo Temple, the Tower of Ra and the Tower of Set, among dozens of other exotic names. A good many people find this annoying or embarrassing, but what else might have been done in so overwhelming a place? A large number of Indian names appear on Canyon maps—Watahomigi Point, Manakaja Point and Paya Point, near the Indian village of Supai—and all honor families who still live there. However, it would not have been possible to use Indian names throughout the Canyon, as has been suggested by some who feel that since the Indians were there first their terms should be the only ones employed. The Indians had no names for many places, and some of the names they did have are too indelicate to be printed on any polite map. A very mild example that is printed is The Maiden's Breast, in the region of Supai.

Continuing down the north Kaibab Trail, the hiker descends the great Redwall Limestone midway between the rim and the river. The Redwall can be followed visually for many miles through the Canyon, a vertical cliff more than 500 feet high that presents a formidable obstacle to rock climbers who venture off the established trails. On the Kaibab, however, ledges have been blasted out that are easy to walk on, although there are one or two straight-down views that may not be to everyone's taste. Wherever the Redwall has been recently scarred it can be seen that it is not red at all, but blue gray. The red color is only a superficial stain that has trickled down from the truly red formations above, the Hermit Shale and Supai Sandstone, which are responsible for staining much of the Canyon below them. The coloring agent is an oxide of iron called hematite. Another iron oxide, limonite, stains the rocks brown in certain strata, buff in others. The Bright Angel Shale is greenish in color because it contains ferrous iron, which also produces various shades of blue.

Not long after descending the Redwall one reaches Bright Angel Creek, which has carved its own tributary canyon along a fault line straight to the Colorado about 11 miles away. The trail becomes very easy and lends itself to the ruminative sort of walking that Thoreau had in mind when he said he had traveled extensively in his own hometown of Concord, Massachusetts.

One of the most arresting features of this part of the Canyon, in fact of almost any part of it below the rim, is the sparse, perfect distribution of plants. It seems Oriental, not in Dutton's Hindu conception, but in a Japanese way. In Japanese gardens, very old ones that have been in the hands of single families for generations, the decision to place or not to place a plant in a certain location may require the lengthiest consideration. The relationship of plants to each other and to the space around them is a matter of great delicacy. And this is exactly the case in the Canyon, save that the decisions are made by nature rather than by an old man in a kimono. It is only in the immediate vicinity of a seep, a spring or a creek—within a few feet—that plants may grow in abundance and confusion. Elsewhere in the stony dryness they must grow singly and fairly far apart or they cannot grow at all. A good illustration of this may be seen by any visitor to the South Rim who looks down at the Tonto Platform, a broad shelf that stretches for miles lengthwise through the Canyon. The Tonto Platform is dotted with burro brush—spreading, bushy shrubs that appear to have been set out by a gardener. Each one grows a considerable and almost identical distance from all its neighbors. In this manner they survive, and new plants do not spring up between them because the far-reaching roots of the mature plants absorb all the available water. A new plant must wait for an old one to die.

As a man walks through the Canyon individual plants, with their special placement, impress themselves on him. He realizes that they are like human beings, alone, solitary, growing where they can, but inextricably connected and bound up with all other similar beings to the farthest reaches of the planet and headed for the same destination. As he looks at them and considers the struggle in which they are engaged, it seems outrageous to him that anyone might think of breaking off their flowers or doing them any injury. According to legend the mandrake plant of Europe and Africa, when it is torn out of the ground, screams.

The most spectacular of the wild flowers along the Kaibab Trail—and it is a wild flower in the sense that the Eiffel Tower is a piece of blacksmithing—is the mescal, also called the agave, maguey or century plant. In general construction it is not unlike an enormous artichoke with hard sawtoothed leaves three or even four feet long. It does not really live for a century, but from 10 to 30 years. It is worth pausing for a while to look at a mescal, not because it is handsome but because of the incredible thing it is someday going to do. All its life it will prepare to bloom, and when it is finally ready it will produce a central bud that may be as big around as a six-by-six timber. The bud becomes a stalk and grows upward at an astonishing and almost visible rate—three, four, perhaps 10 inches a day, until it reaches a height of 10 to 20 feet. Large yellow flowers appear in stemmed clusters at the top of the stalk and then the plant, exhausted, dies.

In numerous places in the Canyon there are rings of fire-blackened stones about 20 feet in diameter. The Kaibab Trail passes very close to one of them—in fact was originally built through it. These are the remains of circular pits in which the Indians used to roast the buds of mescals, which in early summer they collected over a large area and brought together for feasts. The buds, according to those who have eaten them, are sweet, with somewhat the consistency and taste of candied yams. The Indians no longer roast them, it being considerably easier to satisfy a craving for sweets by going to the store for a can of peaches.

At the bottom of the Canyon the trail reaches the Colorado at Phantom Ranch. This privately operated cluster of cabins and restaurant, sometimes jokingly described by the people who run it as "the lowest-down ranch in the world," has existed in its present location since 1922; it was built on the site of a camp established when the cable crossing the river was installed in 1907. Its buildings, fortunately, are old and decrepit and do not offend the wilderness as much as might be expected, although it would be far better if there were no buildings anywhere in any national park except administrative offices and perhaps museums and lecture halls at the entrances.

After crossing the river on a narrow suspension footbridge one turns right on the River Trail, which has been blasted along the very brink of the Inner Gorge above the Colorado. In less than two miles the River Trail reaches the foot of the Bright Angel Trail, where the ascent to the South Rim begins. As one goes up, he moves through the same geological formations and life zones, thinking much the same sort of thoughts.

The creatures that one sees while hiking seem, like the plants, strikingly individual. One of these is the chuckwalla, a large lizard that may attain a length of 18 inches. At a fleeting glance it appears dull brown or slate-colored but, close up, it can be seen to have little yellow and red speckles on its back. The chuckwalla has some notable distinctions. Unlike the majority of reptiles, it is a vegetarian. There are far better places than the Grand Canyon in which to be a vegetarian, but somehow the chuckwalla is there and somehow it exists. The second of its distinctions is its manner of defending itself. When it is frightened it scurries into a rock crevice slightly larger than itself. There it gulps as much air as it can hold, inflating and wedging its body so tightly into the crevice that it is very difficult to pull out. This tactic, translated into human terms, has no doubt been encountered by most people at one time or another. A fat relative, usually an in-law, comes to spend the weekend. But at the end of a month the relative is still in the guest room. What is more, the relative's possessions have proliferated and swollen. There are more suitcases, boxes, clothing and appliances. The relative is wedged in. It can be a great problem.

The Paiute Indians used to eat chuckwallas and still occasionally do. The meat is reported to have a flavor like that of frogs' legs. The Paiutes never had any trouble getting inflated chuckwallas out of crevices. They would take a sharply pointed stick and—poof!—they would puncture their prey and let out all the air. In such matters Indians are smarter than white people.

There is another creature in the Canyon, rarely seen, that is not merely unusual but unique: the pink rattlesnake (actually its color varies from pink to salmon and vermilion). The thought of a solid pink rattlesnake may be discouraging to some hikers, but in fact the reptile is very shy and flees or hides at the approach of people. Its color may be an evolutionary change, an adaptation to the red rocks among which it. lives. It is found only in the Grand Canyon, as its wonderfully apt last name suggests: *Crotalus viridis abyssus*.

As the Bright Angel Trail approaches the South Rim its switchbacks seem to become innumerable. The Coconino Sandstone and Kaibab Limestone are particularly steep at this point, and a man walks perhaps 60 feet in one direction, turns, and walks 60 feet in the opposite direction to make a gain in altitude of 10 feet. On his back he carries everything he brought into the Canyon at the North Rim except the food he has consumed. The park law is, "You packed it in, you pack it out," and this applies even to the smallest of waste items, bits of tinfoil and the filter tips of cigarettes. Sadly, the law is often broken and park employees must spend a good deal of time picking up garbage. In the area of Grand Canyon village they are obliged to go over the rim, dangling on long ropes and risking their lives to collect the candy wrappers, cardboard lunchboxes and the other rubbish of tourists.

Even near the top of the trail it is still possible to see unusual creatures. In June 1941, on this part of the Bright Angel a Russian-born lepidopterist named V. Nabokov captured a previously undiscovered butterfly, a small brown one belonging to the species *Neonympha*. With the aid of a grant from the Museum of Comparative Zoology of Harvard College he published an article describing it in the learned journal *Psyche.* As its discoverer he was privileged to name the butterfly and so he christened it *Neonympha dorothea dorothea,* in honor of a friend who had "kicked it up" as they were walking. He signed his article merely V. Nabokov, but later, when he came to write a celebrated book not about a *Neonympha* but about a nymphet, *Lolita,* he used his full name, Vladimir Nabokov.

After the last of the switchbacks one stands on the Canyon's rim, a little tired, and turns to look back across that enormous gulf. In the slant of the afternoon sun the colors are changing and the temples and buttes are preparing to move stealthily around. The Canyon is filled with its enormous hush. The enchantment is there and will be remembered into old age, perhaps even to the age of 76.

The Spirits of the Chasm

Long before geologists arrived in the Grand Canyon to examine its rocks and deduce its origins, the Indians who lived around the Canyon had created their own explanations for the formation of the spectacular chasm. These ideas, passed down from generation to generation by tribal medicine men and storytellers, were expressed as poetic myths. The beauty and power of these myths are suggested by the excerpts quoted under the pictures of the Canyon region that appear on the following pages.

The Canyon myths are part of broad cosmologies that enabled the Indians to cope with a harsh and unpredictable environment, making comprehensible the forces that surrounded their unique world. To the Ute and the Southern Paiute, the Hualapai and Havasupai, the Hopi and the Navajo, that world and those forces were inextricably joined. Rocks were not simply rocks; they were supernatural beings, watching over the tribesmen and guarding their collective destiny. Water, in that water-starved land, had a life of its own. The great river that formed the Canyon gorge led to the Indians' promised land, and springs had souls, to be placated by offerings of peaches, corn and tobacco.

The animals that the Indian hunted, the spiders that inhabited his dwelling, the snakes that slithered across his trail, all were his equals—sometimes his heroes and sometimes his spiritual mentors.

The spider was wise and gave advice from an inconspicuous spot behind the listener's ear. The coyote was a sage and resourceful being who knew what made the sun rise and set. Thus the Indians made the mysteries of the Canyon—and of their own lives—seem less threatening. But the necessary communication with the spirit world was neither easy nor lightly undertaken. To gain access to its knowledge, the Indians used songs, dances, sorcery —and, occasionally, a hallucinogenic drug, the sacred datura, a plant relative of the tomato and the potato. The datura contains dangerous amounts of atropine (used in modern medicine to treat asthma); indeed, this substance was so potent that the plant was to be chewed only when other forms of divination, such as dreaming and star gazing, had failed. And it was best taken in the company of a good singer, for a strong and expressive voice was believed to be capable of controlling and directing the power of the drug.

To the Indians who chewed it the sacred datura caused "the mind to go around and go out in many directions." This mental liberation enabled man to establish contact with the spirits that lived in animals, plants and rocks.

"If you lose something, eat a piece of datura. Then you'll see it in a dream and when you wake up you can go to it."—Navajo lore

"*Packithaawi struck his knife deep into the water-covered ground, and there the great canyon was soon formed.*"—Hualapai myth

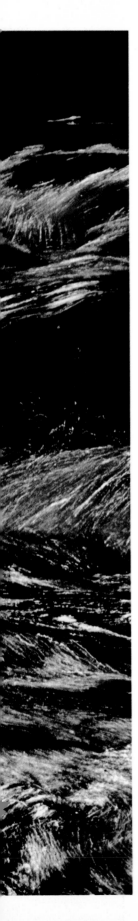

How the "Big Water" Came into Being

Running like a leitmotif through the mythology of the Indians who lived near it, the Colorado River, shown on these pages as seen from the shore at Lava Falls, was too powerful a presence to be ignored. The mere sight of so much water in a dry land must have filled them with awe.

To the Indians, the "big water deep down in earth" seemed to have no end or beginning. A Ute myth says (*excerpt at right*) that the river was created by the god Tavwoats to cover up a trail that led to the irresistible Land of Joy, thereby preventing discontented people from leaving their workaday world. The Navajo, the Hualapai and the Havasupai still believe that the river is the runoff from a great flood that once covered the earth. In the Hualapai myth quoted under the picture at left, the flood was ended by a cult hero named Packithaawi, who smote the ground with a knife and club to create the Grand Canyon. But the Navajo and the Havasupai anticipated modern geologists in their belief that the Canyon was formed by the pressure of the moving water.

"Tavwoats then rolled a raging stream into the gorge."—Ute myth

"He met the Great Snake, the Sun and others who taught him everything."–Hopi myth

How a Hopi Clan Became Snake People

The belief that the river ran down to an underworld was part of a myth that accounted, to many Indians, for their own creation. The Hopi tale accounts for the tribe's affiliation with snakes in this way: an Indian named Tiyo decided to see where the "Big Water" ended, as told in the excerpt quoted under the picture at right. He sealed himself inside a hollowed-out log and drifted down the river to the underworld home of the Hopi gods.

There Tiyo met the snake people, one of whose maidens he married. When he returned from the underworld, his snake wife came along and eventually bore him snake children. Tiyo's fellow villagers, fearing their bite, drove out the snake children—along with their mother. This action offended the gods, and they sent a drought that the Hopi could lift only by welcoming snakes back into the village. Ever since, serpents like the king snake shown at left have been part of a ceremony performed by the Hopi to bring rain. Traditionally the festival climaxes as Tiyo's descendants dance with rattlesnakes in their mouths.

"All day Tiyo would sit at the edge of the cliffs, looking into the deep gorge, wondering where the water went."—Hopi myth

How the Havasupai Became Farmers

High up on a spur of canyon wall that juts into the Havasupai Indian Reservation perch two pillarlike rocks that the Indians call the Wigeleeva (one appears at upper right in this view of Havasu Canyon).

The Wigeleeva have a fateful significance in the past, present and future of the Havasupai. According to the legend that is quoted under the picture, the nomadic ancestors of the tribe chose the verdant canyon as their permanent residence because of the pillars—which they saw as protective spirits looking down on the valley floor. Since the Indians settled down on the stream of blue water, the Wigeleeva have been the tribe's guardians. The Havasupai believe that the Prince and Princess, or God and Goddess—as the twin rocks are sometimes called—preside over their crops (mainly corn, squash and beans) and ensure a good harvest. Indeed, the Havasupai say that if the two rocks should ever fall, as someday they must, the village —and the entire Havasupai people —would cease to exist.

"The god makes our gardens grow. It guards us. If we leave it, we will die. If it falls, our village will be destroyed."—Havasupai myth

5/ People of the Blue-Green Water

Wilderness is not invariably or simply an attribute of the land; it may be in a man's mind too. There are some civilized things in Lemuel J. Paya's mind, others not so civilized. Lemuel J. Paya, whose name is pronounced *PIE-ya,* is a Havasupai Indian who estimates that he is about 75 years old. His face is deeply creased and wrinkled and, when he closes his one good eye and sings in his language, a dialect of the Yuman spoken also by the Yavapai, Hualapai and Tonto Indians of the Southwest, it is difficult to tell exactly where, among all the wrinkles, Paya's eye is until he stops singing and opens it again. Paya's voice ranges up and down a scale Bach never dreamed of; rocking back and forth, he sings to the owner of all the animals.

Paya is in fine shape for his age except for the missing eye. Fifty years ago he was skinning a bobcat and he had hung the carcass up on a tree limb so he could work on it easily. He was using an extremely sharp knife to cut a tendon near one of the bobcat's hind leg joints, working with his face close to the joint so he could see exactly what he was doing. He slipped the blade behind the tendon and pulled it toward him. The tendon resisted, so he gave the blade a harder pull. The tendon suddenly parted and the knife kept coming toward Paya's face. It slashed deep into his left eye, the contents of which came out and ran down his cheek. For years the government doctors have been willing to give Paya a glass or plastic eye but he cannot be bothered.

When Lemuel sings to the owner of all the animals he asks to be allowed to shoot fat deer. As nearly as it can be translated, he sings to someone or something "far up in the buck brush, underneath the north star," asking to be allowed to find and kill deer. Not many of them, just one or two, enough for his needs.

"Who is the owner of all the animals, Mr. Paya? Is it God?"

"No, no. Just the owner." Does he mean the owner is a spirit? Perhaps. The Havasupai Indians, except for a very few who go to the little mission church in their village, are not monotheistic and do not believe much in Christ. Many of them, the older ones particularly, are afraid of ghosts. There is one blind old man who has constructed a sort of horizontal spiderweb of wires and ropes on sticks stuck into the ground outside the door of his hut. One wire leads to where the horse is, another to where the firewood is, and one leads to the privy. The old man will not go out after dark, feeling his way along the wire to the privy, unless his wife goes along too, because a ghost might get him.

There are other Indians who live on the plateau above the Grand Canyon, but the Havasupai are the only ones who make their homes in the Canyon itself. Their name means "people of the blue-green water," and they are perhaps the smallest numerically and certainly the most isolated tribe of Indians in this country. About 300 of them live in a side canyon, called Havasu Canyon on some maps and Cataract Canyon on others, near the bottom of the Grand Canyon, on a reservation of 518.6 acres. All of the Havasupai except the youngest children have been up on the plateau to see the civilization of the white man, whom they call *haigu*. The Indians wear *haigu's* clothes, speak *haigu's* language when need be, and use his mail-order catalogues in their outhouses. There is nothing in history, custom or treaty, however, that obliges them to love *haigu,* and they do not. On the other hand, they have always been peaceful and long-suffering; they say that they have never killed a white man and that is probably true.

The Indians call themselves Supai for short, and Supai is also the name of their village. They are fairly light-skinned, not red; lion-colored might be more accurate. They are of stocky build and almost all the women tend toward fat, though they remain physically strong. A few years ago their average life expectancy was only 44, but recently the efforts of the U.S. Public Health Service have increased it somewhat. As young children they are very attractive and appealing, with bright, anthracite eyes and a manner of offering affection with impulsive hugs, expecting to be hugged immediately in return.

Although there are various horse- and foot-trails down into Havasu Canyon, the best way of getting there is to follow Route 66 toward Peach Springs, Arizona. Seven miles east of Peach Springs, take a dirt road that wanders 63 miles northeast across the Coconino Plateau. This road, sometimes impassable after heavy rains, leads to Hualapai Hilltop, which is not a town but a jumping-off place. Arrangements can be made by mail or telephone—a wire goes down to the village of Supai through the switchboard of Prescott, Arizona—to rent a horse for about $20 round trip. From Hualapai Hilltop, it is an eight-mile ride into Supai, 2,000 feet below. Most visitors walk, carrying a backpack. Passing through the Indian reservation, on the way to a campground beyond it on national parkland, you must pay the Indians a modest fee of $2.

The descent begins sharply, along grayish sandstone slopes patched with blackbrush, junipers and mesquite, and the valley is wide. But soon the cliffs on both sides rise higher, hundreds of feet, and press closer together. The valley becomes a canyon and then a gorge and then, in places, a very deep, narrow, winding corridor full of shadows from whose depths only a handbreadth of sky is visible. The enclosing cliffs change color, becoming a rich brownish red, and in the dry heat one thinks of a brickkiln or of some alternate route that might be used when the turnpike to hell is closed for repairs. But then after one of its many turns the canyon begins to widen and the air becomes cooler. Another turn, another, and there appears an astonishing sight: the fresh, breeze-tossed green of cottonwoods and willows and the gleam of moving water. Havasu Creek, which has a flow of about 28,200 gallons a minute, has come up out of the floor of the thirsting canyon as though Moses had struck the ground with his rod.

Like Havasu, most of the side canyons that empty into the Grand Canyon have been—and are still being—gullied out by streams fed by rain or snow on the plateaus above. When there is particularly heavy precipitation up there, the chocolate-colored water gushes and foams down the side canyons, yelling and rejoicing to join the mighty Colorado. But when there is no rain or snowmelt, which is most of the time, not a few of the side canyons are dry and still. Little lizards and yellow scorpions and various cacti live in them. Everything, to survive, must bite, prick or sting, and the sound of life is a slither. But Havasu Canyon, from the place where the creek emerges to the point of its juncture with the Colorado, a distance of about 10 miles, is never dry.

The Coconino Plateau, through which Havasu Canyon is carved, stretches southward from the rim of the Grand Canyon. The plateau is

Lemuel J. Paya, who lost his left eye while skinning a bobcat, is an elder of the Havasupai, a small, isolated Indian tribe in the Canyon. Once chairman of the Supai Tribal Council, Paya retains a role as spokesman, explaining to visitors such tribal skills as tanning a hide or making a deer stand still—by carrying a talisman, a deer's calculus.

formed of porous limestone; rainwater seeps down through it to considerable depths. Oozing and trickling underground in an enormous trellis-shaped pattern, the water makes its way toward Havasu. It is thought that a large part of the plateau, from the San Francisco Peaks on the east to Mount Floyd and Bill Williams Mountain on the west, an area of about 3,500 square miles, is drained in this manner. The water emerges in Havasu at the point where the canyon becomes deep enough to encounter the water-bearing stratum. Once above ground, the stream goes rollicking through the Indian reservation, which occupies an irregularly shaped, flat area on the canyon floor about four miles long but quite narrow, the red cliffs being only a few hundred yards apart.

In its subterranean travels Havasu Creek absorbs a good many chemical compounds, among them calcium sulfate, magnesium carbonate and calcium carbonate. These have little effect on the taste of the water, which is fine, but they are responsible for the dramatic blue color of the creek. When it first comes out of the floor of the canyon, Havasu Creek is of no particular color, but it soon becomes turquoise. There are many parts of the ocean, notably in the Caribbean, where the water is of a similar blue. But who has seen a fresh-water creek, only about 20 feet wide and two or three feet deep, that makes the sky itself seem pale? Actually, the Caribbean and Havasu Creek get their brilliant hue from the same trick of light on a white bottom—sand or coral in the case of the ocean, sediment from the carbonates in the case of the creek: the blue of the sky is reflected by the bottom up through the water. The deeper the water, the deeper the color; there are pools near the lower end of Havasu Creek so blue that while the eye delights in them the mind keeps stubbornly saying, "This is not true"; held in a cup or seen tumbling over a cascade, the creek's waters are colorless.

Several miles from the border of the Indian reservation there begins a series of four magnificent waterfalls down which the creek plunges, blue and clear, into the Colorado. The blue is not as intense as it is in the pools because the water cascades in relatively thin sheets, but they are colorful enough. The highest of the four, at about 200 feet, is called Mooney Falls and takes its name not from an Indian chief, brave or maid, but from an Irishman, James Mooney. That unlucky man, who had been a sailor and learned something (but not enough) about ropes, came to Arizona in the last century to hunt for valuable minerals. In 1880 he ventured into Havasu Canyon with a few companions and came to the brink of the towering waterfall. He wished to descend the cliff be-

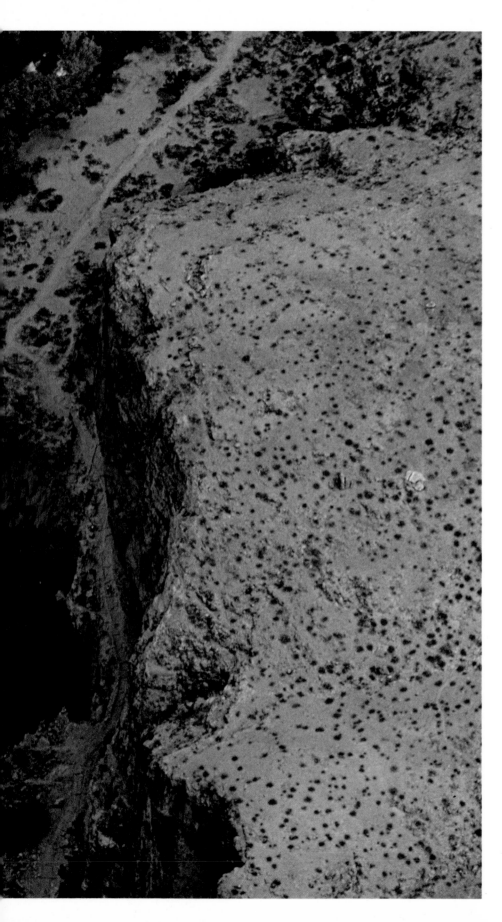

Havasu Falls, one in a series of four falls along Havasu Creek, plummets 100 feet between Havasu Canyon's red walls into a pool. Chemicals in the water—which in part account for its remarkable blue-green color—also produce the filmy curtains of travertine that hang from every surface touched by the fall's spray; as the spray evaporates, the chemical residue turns to stone. Along the moist banks are cottonwood, willow, wild grape and watercress, providing a dense haven for cormorants, hummingbirds and mallards, as well as rock squirrel, beaver and bighorn sheep. The upper end of the stream waters the 518-acre Havasupai Indian Reservation, turning the canyon floor into a lush oasis.

side the falls, and so asked his companions to lower him on the end of a 150-foot-long rope. The mathematical fact is that 200 minus 150 leaves 50. Because of the roaring of the water, Mooney could not tell his companions to pull him up and for some reason he could not climb back up himself. According to one story, he dangled for two days before letting go. Several months later his friends returned with longer ropes, found Mooney's body on the rocks beside the falls and buried him. The Indians, who had previously referred to the falls as "Mother of the Waters," soon took to calling them Mooney Falls. This would seem to be a great honor to the late *haigu,* although one cannot always tell what Indians are thinking.

There are some mineral deposits in the neighborhood of the falls, principally of calcite and vanadinite—the ores from which quicklime and vanadium are refined. Though some small mines have been dug there, no one has profited much; the cost of transporting heavy ore out of that place is too great. Of greater interest are the minerals in the water of the creek itself. When it hardens, calcium carbonate forms a limestone called travertine, which is often used for construction—many of the great buildings of Renaissance and Baroque Rome, including St. Peter's, are made of travertine. In its modest but curious way Havasu Creek does some building as well. Near the falls its water, laden with calcium carbonate, fills the air with spray and mist that are blown against the cliff walls. When the water evaporates it leaves an infinitesimal film of travertine; and in this manner, during thousands of years, the cliffs have been hung with huge, tattered curtains of stone. Travertine also builds up on bits of vegetation beside the creek. Here and there near the falls one can find a blade of grass or even a flower that is slowly being, in the words of the hymnist, sealed in a stone-cold tomb.

The most obvious of all the effects of Havasu Creek upon the canyon is to make it luxuriantly green. The cottonwoods and willows at first catch the eye because of their height, but beneath them are box elders, hackberry trees and wild-grape vines. Along the creek are arrowweed, watercress, maidenhair ferns, cattails and the crimson flecks of monkey flowers. Flashing in the greenness are many colorful birds—in summer, bright red tanagers, white-throated swifts, violet-green swallows, yellow warblers, hummingbirds, goldfinches and exquisite little lazuli buntings, feathered in blue with brown breasts. The pools in the creek attract grebes, cormorants, kingfishers, green-winged teals and great blue herons.

The extraordinary combination of colors—the red cliffs and the bright green vegetation, the turquoise water and the blue sky—creates an effect that is both beautiful and eerie, like a landscape by a greatly gifted primitive painter. This effect is especially strong in the region of the waterfalls—and the major falls, including Mooney, lie beyond the Indian reservation, down the canyon toward the Colorado. When the reservation was laid out in the 1880s, the Indians were asked what the boundaries of their country should be. Ko-hót, the Havasupai chief, told the cavalry officers representing the government that he was afraid that too large a tract would be encroached on—perhaps taken away altogether. He therefore asked for only enough land to maintain the farming the Indians had been practicing along the creek for about 1,000 years. They didn't need the falls for that.

When Ko-hót hedged his bet, farming provided only half the Indians' livelihood. From spring until fall they lived in the canyon growing corn, melons, beans and squash. Prudently, they dried part of their crop and stored it in carefully sealed caves in the cliff walls. Then, with the onset of winter, the entire tribe moved out of the canyon and went up to the plateau. There they lived by gathering seeds and pine nuts, and by hunting deer and antelope across hundreds of square miles. If the hunting was bad, they returned to the canyon to pick up some of their stored food, but apparently they were excellent hunters and it was not often necessary for them to draw on their caches in the cliffs. This seasonal arrangement was ideal. But when the *haigu* arrived with his cattle and his fences he crowded the game off the plateau, thus cutting the Indians' way of life in half. Today the crops on the canyon floor—only about 150 acres are arable—cannot sustain the tribe, and if an Indian wishes to shoot a deer or an antelope on his ancestral hunting grounds, he cannot do it when he is hungry but must obtain a license and wait until the white man tells him the season is open. Consequently, most of the Indians are undernourished, fall sick easily, and are living on welfare, government-surplus food and what little they can earn by guiding tourists into their canyon on horseback. However, it is not in the province of this book to deal with their condition or the injustices done them, but with the wilderness that survives in them.

Lemuel J. Paya was talking about what he liked to eat (when he could get it), and he mentioned rabbit soup. He described how "you skin the rabbit and gut it but leave the head on, and boil it for a long time. Occasionally you look into the pot, where the rabbit's eyes are staring up at you, and when the meat is about to fall off the bones, you throw in several handfuls of crushed pine nuts, shells included, and bring the liquid to a boil again. The soup is delicious and the bones and the thick stuff in the bottom of the pot are much liked by dogs."

Paya himself has not shot a deer for three years; the vision in his remaining eye is "getting a little smoky." However, he has accompanied his sons when they went hunting upon the plateau, and has sung to the owner of all the animals on their behalf. "You look around, find two little white shiny stones, put them in your cheeks, and begin to sing. Pretty soon you see a deer."

"Does this work?" one of Paya's sons was asked.

"Of course," he said. He seemed to find the question ridiculous.

"Another thing that's good luck in hunting deer is a charm stone you find in a deer's belly," Paya went on. He meant a calculus, a hard lump that in humans might be a gallstone or kidney stone. "Once in a long, long time, very seldom, you find a stone inside a deer. Keep it. Carry it in your pocket when you hunt, and it charms the deer. They just stand still and look at you when you come up to them."

For centuries the Havasupai Indians produced the best and whitest tanned buckskins in the Southwest; these were their mainstay in intertribal trade. Today very few such skins are produced—there is little demand for them among Indians, and white people can buy factory-made, simulated buckskin leather garments in Sears, Roebuck. Lemuel Paya still knows how to make the genuine article. It happens that deer (and various other animals) are outfitted with the very chemicals necessary to tan their own hides. The chemicals are contained in the deer's brain and the marrow of its spinal column.

"After you soak the hide in the creek a day and a night, you scrape the hair off and you dry it and stretch it. To tan it you cook the brain, mash it up good in water, and spray it all over the hide with your mouth. Squeeze the hide to work the brain into it pretty good, let it dry a while, and then you take the marrow from the spine and boil that, and do the same thing. Of course there's other steps to it, rubbing and wringing it out, but that's the main thing, the brain and the spinal."

"How do you scrape the hair off?"

"Well, white people, they might use a knife and make a lot of nicks and cuts in the hide. The right thing is to use the sharp rib of a horse. It's curved, and you put the hide over a log with the bark peeled off, very smooth, and scrape it with the rib. Nowadays you can use a piece of stovepipe instead of a log, it's even smoother."

Anachronisms are everywhere. Supai has a little post office, the last post office in the United States that is served by packtrain. Three times a week an Indian takes a string of horses up to the rim of the Grand Canyon to get the mail and supplies like bread and canned stew that come by parcel post. It is a vision out of the 19th or even the 18th Century to see the pack horses coming down along the cliffs to the post office: Supai, Arizona, zip code 86435.

Objects that are too heavy for pack horses are brought in by helicopter. The U.S. Marines used one of their big cargo lifters a while ago to fetch in a small yellow bulldozer and a tractor. The Bureau of Indian Affairs, prodded by various angry and well-intentioned Arizonans seeking to ease the hard life of the Indians, has lately been airlifting prefabricated houses, in sections, into the canyon. The houses look grossly out of place on the green floor between the red cliffs.

Lemuel J. Paya lives in one of the new houses with assorted members of his family. He has been officially married twice, and when he recently counted them, he had 22 grandchildren. One of the virtues of the new houses is that they have several rooms. Most of the other Havasupai live in one- or two-room shacks; living in such close quarters and following the example of their elders, the children start serious sex play at the age of eight or nine. The illegitimacy rate is high, although divorce is not as common as might be supposed. The Indians, at least nominally, follow the white man's law in such matters, but divorce may simply be de facto after angry arguments and declarations, as is the case in many tribes. Among the Navajo, who live up on the rim of the Grand Canyon to the east of the Havasupai, a woman may divorce her husband merely by putting his saddle outside the door of their hogan.

The Havasupai have a judge, whom they elect; he adjudicates minor cases, almost always involving strong drink. (It is a federal crime to take liquor onto the Indian reservation, but the Havasupai often smuggle it in.) They also have a jail with a flush toilet, built for them by the Bureau of Indian Affairs. A recently elected judge was a woman, who like all of her fellow Havasupai had scant formal education. Her legal credentials were that she had passed some time upon the plateau working as a servant for some white people and had watched *Divorce Court* on television a good many times.

Television has not come to the bottom of Havasu Canyon, and it may not come for a long time, since broadcast signals are not easily received so far below the rim. But even without it, the Indians' sense of their identity as a people has been seriously damaged by the entertainment industry. When the weekly movie shown in Supai (paid for by B.I.A. funds) is a Western—and it frequently is—the little Supai children cheer loudly as the U.S. cavalry arrives in the nick of time to rout the wicked Indians. Yet not long ago one Supai boy, in whom the old aboriginal spark was burning with surprising vigor, said to a visiting white man, "I want to be an Indian when I grow up."

Mainly, however, it is among the old that the wilderness can still be glimpsed. It survives most tenaciously in customs connected with birth, religion and death. An old woman, usually the maternal grandmother, is often in attendance at the birth of a baby, if the mother has not taken the option offered to her by the U.S. Public Health Service to have the baby in a hospital up on the plateau. The woman ties the umbilical cord about an inch and a half from the baby's body, then cuts it on the far side of the tie and dusts the stump with powdered red ocher. (The ocher, a bright red earthy substance, a form of iron ore, comes from a secret place known to the old Indians. The ocher was once a valuable trade item; other tribes prized it to make paint for their faces. On babies' umbilical cords it does no harm.) The woman then runs her fingers all over the baby's face, head and body, like a sculptor, to ensure that when the child grows up it will be handsome and well formed.

When the remaining bit of umbilical cord dries and drops off, the old lady wraps it in a bit of cloth and fastens it to the head of the baby's cradle. After about a year, in a rare survival of an ancient ritual, the remnant of cord is ground up, mixed with red ocher, and made into a paint by blending the mixture with fat—preferably that of a deer. The cord is then "returned" to the child in three lines of paint. One line begins at the tip of his middle finger, goes up his arm, across his shoulders and down to the tip of the opposite middle finger. Another extends from one armpit down the side of the body and leg, crosses the sole of the foot, goes up the inner side of the leg to the crotch, and continues in like manner until the other armpit is reached. The third line is painted from the hairline on the forehead straight down the nose, chin and body, under the crotch and up the back to the nape of the neck. It is thought, at least by the old, that if this ritual is not performed the child may grow up to be troublesome and absent-minded.

Among old men—and indeed among the younger, who enjoy its pleasurable aspects without acknowledging that anything remotely religious is involved—the sweat lodge is still an important institution. Once almost universal among the North American Indians, the sweat lodge has remained essentially the same among the Havasupai since it was de-

veloped many hundreds of years ago as a place for purifying the body
and propitiating spirits. The lodge is dome-shaped, six or seven feet in
diameter and about four feet high, framed with bent poles, thatched
with willow brush and plastered with earth. It contains an opening
large enough to admit a man; the opening was closed with skins until recent times, when canvas or old blankets became available. Stones are
heated in a fire nearby, and when they have become fiercely hot they
are placed in a pit within the lodge, formerly with greenwood tongs but
now with a long-handled shovel. Then, wearing only breechcloths, three
or four men enter the lodge and close the door. Water is sprinkled on
the hot stones, turning instantly to steam, and the temperature soon
rises as high as 150°. A white man in the sweat lodge among the Indians in the blistering-hot darkness is likely to feel a sense of his own
not-so-remote wildness. The feeling becomes more intense when Lemuel J. Paya, as the senior man present, begins to sing. This time he sings
a sort of prayer or petition asking that the aches and pains of his companions and himself may be relieved.

After about ten minutes the men emerge, lie down on the sand for a
while, and then reenter the sweat lodge. Four steamings, separated by
rest periods, are considered sufficient. After the fourth, the men plunge
into the cool water of Havasu Creek, discovering that Paya's prayer
has been answered.

The Havasupai religion has never developed in any systematic way.
On rare occasions the Indians may pray to the sun, trees, rocks, the
wind, water and the earth—but not to a specific god who might inhabit
them. On a promontory that juts out from the cliff wall into their canyon there are two irregular red pillars left by a freak of erosion. From
the ground, these stones appear to be about 10 feet in diameter and perhaps 40 feet tall, precariously perched. They are called the Wigeleeva
and are said by some to be a god and goddess. But no one pays them rev-
erence. Paya says they represent the petrified remains of two brothers,
tribal chiefs of long ago, who led the Indians into Havasu Canyon and
are still standing guard over them. Some of the older Indians say that
when the Wigeleeva fall down the world will end. Time and further erosion will inevitably topple them, unless the sonic boom of some passing
aircraft does so first.

Havasupai funeral customs reflect ancient traditions and superstit-
tions. When a Havasupai dies his house is abandoned for several weeks;
in former times it was burned. If the dead man owned a few peach, al-

mond, fig or pomegranate trees, one or two of them may be cut down; in the old days all might have been cut, and the man's crops destroyed as well. There is no grasping for the possessions of the deceased, but rather a shunning of them. It is felt that a man's ghost lingers near his things; anyone who touches them may be carried off by the ghost to be his companion in death.

Homer Manakaja, whose family name is pronounced *ma-na-KAY-ja,* died at the age of 27. He had gone up to the plateau to escort a little Havasupai girl to a hospital; she had hepatitis. On the way back from the hospital Homer was riding in the front seat of an ambulance with the driver, a white man, and both were killed in a head-on crash. Homer was embalmed and put in a coffin at government expense, but the Indians had to scrape together $200 to hire a helicopter to carry him down into Supai for burial.

The coffin was placed in the Indians' meeting hall with Manakaja's head to the northwest in accord with ancient prescription. At nightfall the adults of the tribe gathered to mourn him, and during all the dark hours they took turns in a slow, undulating dance around the coffin. Occasionally one of the women would loose a howling wail of grief, setting off a chorus of wails that could be heard far down the canyon. In the middle of the night they opened the coffin and looked at the dead man.

In the morning the coffin was closed and placed inside a large, specially made wooden crate. And then, on top of the coffin and around it inside the crate, the mourners placed things that had belonged to Homer Manakaja as well as things of their own that they wished to give to his ghost as propitiatory presents. Homer's saddle went into the crate, and a pair of boots—not cheap or worn-out boots but a new pair that had cost $70. There was food and money and a good set of carpenter's tools, shirts, factory-made and hand-woven Navajo blankets. Then the crate was nailed shut.

Although some of the Havasupai families bury their dead in out-of-the-way corners of the canyon, the main burial ground is near the reservation boundary and the first of the waterfalls below the village, and it was there that they took Manakaja. The lone tractor in Supai pulled the crate along the narrow trail and soon, if one looked back, it was no longer possible to see any of the things that *haigu* had brought into the canyon, not the prefab houses, the store, the post office or the jail, but only the flashing blue water, the red cliffs and the greenness of the trees and plants beside the water. The Indians followed along, one of them leading a horse that had been Homer Manakaja's. The older Indians paid little heed to the horse but the younger ones, who knew what was going to happen to the animal (but had never seen such a thing), kept eying it.

The burial ground is among rocks and sand below the red cliff at the right of the trail with the stream on the left. There are no carved gravestones or noticeable markers; visitors who pass on their way from the village to the national park campground are rarely aware that they are within a few yards of a cemetery. The pit that had been dug for Homer's crate was ready, but at the last moment it was found to be too small. While a few volunteers enlarged the pit, the Indians glanced uneasily around them; even during the day, they are uncomfortable in the burial ground. When the pit had been sufficiently enlarged, the crate was lowered into it and some of the men began shoveling sand onto it.

Others were preparing to sacrifice Homer Manakaja's horse—so that he might have the use of it wherever he was going. There are various traditional ways of killing a horse at or near a Havasupai grave. Since the horse suspects no harm, it can be led to the brink of a cliff and there, by a sudden concerted effort of several men, pushed over the edge. This method has been used within the lifetime of Lemuel J. Paya. Another method is to drive a heavy, sharp knife into a vital spot near the back of the horse's head.

Homer Manakaja's horse was led off a short distance from the grave and shot, a method that will probably continue to be used in the future. Although not traditional, it spares trouble. When the horse was dead and the grave covered, the Indians departed. At various times in the following weeks they returned in small groups to decorate the grave. The Indians had sent out by mail for plastic flowers—roses, peonies, tulips, carnations, daffodils—and when these were delivered by pack horse the mourners ventured into the burial ground to stick them into Homer Manakaja's mound of sand. The plastic flowers, being fairly durable and conspicuous, may remain for quite a while to catch the visitor's eye and he may walk over to examine them, thinking how civilized the wilderness has become. If he happens to notice the jumbled skeleton of a large animal nearby, he may wonder what it died of.

Exploring the "Fretful River"

The first expedition to explore the upper Colorado River and the gorge of the Grand Canyon began hundreds of miles upstream from the Canyon at Green River Station, Wyoming—the railroad depot closest to the Colorado River system. Here, in late May of 1869, nine hardy adventurers—hunters and tough former soldiers—carefully completed preparations under the watchful eye of their leader, John Wesley Powell.

Powell, a dedicated teacher and scientist, had returned from the Civil War with the rank of major—and without his right arm. Powell more than offset this handicap with assets of knowledge and experience. His earlier summertime expeditions through the Rockies had made him, at the age of 35, a seasoned explorer, a budding authority on the Indians and a capable geologist.

Powell was also a skilled organizer and promoter. To mount his private expedition, he raised funds from universities, cadged supplies from the Army and persuaded the Union Pacific to provide free transportation to Green River Station for his men and their Chicago-built boats. (The boats were named *Emma Dean*, after Powell's wife, *Maid of the Canyon, Kitty Clyde's Sister* and, when inspiration failed, *No Name.*) On May 24, the expedition started down the river.

Powell's journal of the three-month journey is adapted on the following pages and illustrated with engravings that appeared when the account was first published in 1875. It told of harrowing rapids, capsized boats, lost supplies and constant toil. Within six weeks, one man, weary of misfortune, took refuge at an Indian agency near the river. Much later, in the depths of the Grand Canyon itself, three more men abandoned the expedition, only to be killed by Indians. Finally, on August 29, two battered boats, carrying six half-starved men, emerged from the Grand Canyon into safe waters.

Powell made a second Canyon voyage two years later; this trip was better equipped and more productive scientifically. But Powell nurtured a special feeling for the companions of his first wild journey. As he wrote in 1895, "The memory of the men and their heroic deeds, the men and their generous acts, overwhelms me with a joy that seems almost a grief."

Major John Wesley Powell, portrayed at right three decades after his first expedition down the Colorado, headed the U.S. Geological Survey for 13 years. Powell also served for 23 years as director of the Bureau of Ethnology, a federal agency established in 1879 to study Indian language and culture.

A Canyon Journal

POWELL'S PARTY SETTING OUT FROM GREEN RIVER STATION

May 24—The good people of Green River City turn out to see us start. We push the four little boats from shore, and the river's swift current carries us down.

During the afternoon we run down to a point where the river sweeps the foot of an overhanging cliff, and here we camp for the night. The sun is yet two hours high, so I climb the cliffs and walk back among the strangely carved rocks of the Green River badlands. These are sandstones and shales, gray and buff, red and brown, blue and black strata in numerous alternations, lying nearly horizontal, and almost without soil and vegetation.

Standing on a high point, I can look off in every direction over a vast landscape, with salient rocks and cliffs glittering in the evening sun. Dark shadows are settling in the valleys and gulches, and the heights are made higher and the depths deeper by the glamor and witchery of light and shade. Away to the south the Uinta Mountains stretch in a long line, high peaks thrust into the sky, and snow fields glittering like lakes of molten silver, and pine forests in somber green. Now the sun goes down, and I return to camp.

Into the Canyon

May 30—This morning we are ready to enter the mysterious canyon, and start with some anxiety. The old mountaineers tell us that it cannot be run; the Indians say, "Water heap catch 'em"; but all are eager for the trial, and off we go.

Entering Flaming Gorge, we quickly run through it on a swift current and emerge into a little park. Half a mile below, the river wheels sharply to the left and enters another canyon cut into the mountain. We enter the narrow passage. On either side the walls rapidly increase in altitude. On the left are overhanging ledges and cliffs—500, 1,000, 1,500 feet high. On the right the rocks are broken and ragged, and the water fills the channel from cliff to cliff.

Now the river turns abruptly around a point to the right, and the waters plunge swiftly down among great rocks; and here we have our first experience with canyon rapids. I stand up in my boat to seek a way among the wave-beaten rocks.

All untried as we are, the moment fills us with intense anxiety. Soon our boats reach the swift current; a stroke or two, now on this side, now on that, and we thread the narrow passage with exhilarating velocity, mounting the high waves, whose foaming crests dash over us, and plunging into the troughs, until we reach the quiet water below. Then comes a feeling of great relief. Our first rapid is run.

A Succession of Rapids

June 8—We enter the Canyon of Lodore, and until noon find a succession of rapids, over which our boats have to be taken. The Canyon of Lodore is 20¾ miles in length. It starts abruptly at what we have called the Gate of Lodore, with walls nearly 2,000 feet high, and they are never lower than this until we reach Alcove Brook, about three miles above the foot of the canyon.

The walls here are very irregular, standing in vertical or overhanging cliffs in places, terraced in others, or receding in steep slopes, and are broken by many side gulches and canyons. The highest point on the wall is Dunn's Cliff, near Triplet Falls, where the rocks reach an altitude of 2,700 feet, but the peaks a little way back rise nearly 1,000 feet higher. Yellow pines, nut pines, firs, and cedars stand in extensive forests on the Uinta Mountains, and, clinging to the rocks and growing in the crevices, come down the walls to the water's edge from Flaming

GATEWAY TO LODORE CANYON

Gorge to Echo Park. The red sandstones are lichened over; delicate mosses grow in the moist places, and ferns festoon the walls.

A Watch on the Channel

June 9—Very slowly we make our way, often climbing on the rocks at the edge of the water for a few hundred yards to examine the channel before running it. During the afternoon we come to a place where it is necessary to make a portage. I land the little boat and the others are signaled to come up.

I walk along the bank to examine the ground, leaving one of my men with a flag to guide the other boats to the landing place. A minute after, I hear a shout, and, looking around, see one of the boats shooting down the center of the fall. It is the *No Name*. I feel that its going over is inevitable, and run to save the third

SCOUTING THE GREEN RIVER BADLANDS

boat. A minute more, and she turns the point and heads for shore. Then I turn down the stream again and scramble along to look for the boat that has gone over. The first fall is not great, only 10 or 12 feet, and we often run such; but below, the river tumbles down again for 40 or 50 feet, in a narrow, angry channel filled with dangerous rocks that break the waves into whirlpools and beat them into white foam.

Loss of a Boat

I pass around a great crag just in time to see the boat strike a rock and, rebounding from the shock, careen and fill its open compartment with water. Two of the men lose their oars; the boat swings around and is carried down at a rapid rate, broadside on, for a few yards, when, striking amidship on another rock with great force, she is broken in two and the men are thrown into the river. But the larger part of the boat floats buoyantly, and they seize it, and down the river they drift, past the rocks for a few hundred yards, to a second rapid filled with huge boulders, where the boat strikes again and is dashed to pieces, and the men and fragments are soon carried beyond my sight.

Running along, I turn a bend and see a man's head above the water, washed about in a whirlpool below a great rock. It is Frank Goodman, clinging to a rock with a grip upon which life depends. Coming opposite, I see Captain Howland trying to go to his aid from an island onto

THE WRECK OF THE NO NAME

which he has been washed. Soon he comes near enough to reach Frank with a pole, which he extends toward him. The latter lets go the rock, grasps the pole, and is then pulled ashore. Seneca Howland, the captain's brother, is washed farther down the island and is caught by some rocks, and, though somewhat bruised, also manages to get ashore.

And now the three men are on an island, with a swift, dangerous river on either side and a fall below. The *Emma Dean* is brought down, and Jack Sumner, starting above as far as possible, pushes out. Right skillfully he plies the oars, and a few strokes set him on the island at the proper point. Then they all pull the boat upstream as far as they are able, until they stand in water up to their necks. One sits on a rock and holds the boat until the others are ready to pull, then gives the boat a push, clings to it with his hands, and climbs in as they pull for mainland, which they reach in safety. We are as glad to shake hands with them as though they had been on a voyage around the world and wrecked on a distant coast.

A Sudden Conflagration

June 16—Late in the afternoon we make a short run to the mouth of another little creek, coming down from the left into an alcove filled with luxuriant vegetation. Here camp is made, with a group of cedars on one side and a dense mass of box elders and dead willows on the other.

I go up to explore the alcove.

A RUNAWAY CAMPFIRE

While I am away a whirlwind comes up and scatters the fire among the dead willows and cedar spray, and soon there is a conflagration. The men rush for the boats, leaving all they cannot readily seize at the moment, and even then they have their clothing burned and hair singed, and Bradley has his ears scorched. The cook fills his arms with the mess kit, and jumping into a boat, stumbles and falls, and away go our cooking utensils into the river. Our plates are gone; our spoons are gone; our knives and forks are gone: "Water catch 'em; h-e-a-p catch 'em."

When on the boats, the men are compelled to cut loose, as the flames, running out on the overhanging willows, are scorching them. Just below is a rapid, filled with rocks. On the shoot, no channel explored, no signal to guide them! Just at this juncture I chance to see them, but I, up in the alcove, have not yet discovered the fire, and the strange movements of the men fill me with astonishment. Down the rocks I clamber, and run to the bank. When I arrive they have landed. Then we all go back to the late camp to see if anything can be saved. Some of the clothing and bedding taken out of the boats is found, also a few tin cups, basins and a camp kettle; and this is all the mess kit we now have. Yet we do just as well as ever.

June 17—Notwithstanding our disasters and toils, we run down to the mouth of the Yampa River. The Yampa enters the Green River from the east. At a point opposite its mouth the Green runs to the south, at the foot of a rock about 700 feet high

POWELL RESCUED BY BRADLEY

and about a mile long, and then turns sharply around the rock to the right and runs back in a northerly course parallel to its former direction for nearly another mile, thus having the opposite sides of a long narrow rock for its bank. The tongue of rock so formed is a peninsular precipice with a mural escarpment along its whole course on the east, but broken down at places in the west.

Trapped at the Top

June 18—We have named the long peninsular rock on the other side Echo Rock. Bradley and I climb it until we have ascended 600 or 800 feet when we are met by a sheer precipice. Looking about, we find a place where it seems possible to climb. I go ahead; Bradley follows until we are nearly to the summit. Here, by making a spring, I gain a foothold in a little crevice, and grasp a rock overhead. I find I can get up no farther and cannot step back, for I dare not let go with my hand and cannot reach a foothold below without letting go. I call to Bradley for help. He finds a way to the top of the rock over my head, but cannot reach me. Standing on my toes, my muscles begin to tremble. If I lose my hold I shall fall to the bottom.

At this instant it occurs to Bradley to take off his long drawers, and he swings them down to me. I hug the rock, seize the dangling legs, and with his assistance gain the top.

July 8—We pass through a region of the wildest desolation. The canyon is very tortuous, and many lateral canyons enter on either side. Piles of broken rock lie against the walls; crags and peaks are seen everywhere. We are minded to call this the Canyon of Desolation.

July 21—We start this morning on the Colorado. The river is rough, and bad rapids in close succession are found. Two very hard portages are made during the forenoon.

July 23—On starting, we come at once to difficult rapids and falls, and so we name this Cataract Canyon.

August 3—Start early this morning. The river, sweeping around bends, undermines the high cliffs in places. Sometimes the rocks are overhanging; in the curves, curious, narrow glens are found.

AT A MONUMENT ROCK—GLEN CANYON

Other wonderful features are the many side canyons or gorges that we pass. On the walls, and back many miles into the country, numbers of monument-shaped buttes are observed. From which of these features shall we select a name? We decide to call it Glen Canyon.

Walls of Polished Marble

August 9—And now the scenery is on a grand scale. The walls of the canyon, 2,500 feet high, are of marble, of many beautiful colors, often polished below by the waves, and sometimes far up the sides, where showers have washed sands over the cliffs. At one place I have walked for more than a mile on a marble pavement, all polished and fretted with strange devices and embossed in fantastic patterns. Through a cleft in the wall the sun shines on this pavement and it gleams in iridescent beauty. As this great bed of marble a thousand feet in thickness forms a distinctive feature of the canyon, we call it Marble Canyon.

The river is now quiet; the canyon wider. Above, when the river is at flood, the waters gorge up, so that the difference between the high-water mark and low-water mark is often 50 or even 70 feet. Sometimes there is a narrow flood plain between the water and the wall. Here we discover mesquite shrubs—small trees with divided leaves and pods.

August 10—Walls still higher; waters swift again. We pass several broad, rugged canyons on our right,

MIDDAY INTERVAL IN MARBLE CANYON

VIEW FROM THE MOUTH OF THE LITTLE COLORADO

and up through these we catch brief glimpses of a forest-clad plateau, miles away to the west.

At 2 o'clock we reach the mouth of the Colorado Chiquito (Little Colorado). This stream enters through a canyon on a scale quite as grand as the Colorado itself. It is a very small river and exceedingly muddy and saline. I walk up the stream three or four miles this afternoon. On my way back I kill two rattlesnakes, and find on my arrival that another has just been killed at camp.

August 11—We remain at this point today, determining the latitude and longitude, measuring the height of the walls, drying our rations, and repairing our boats.

Into the Grand Canyon

August 13—We are now ready to start on our way down the Great Unknown. Our boats, tied to a common stake, chafe each other as they are tossed by the fretful river. They ride high and buoyant, for their loads are lighter than we could desire. We have but a month's rations left.

We are imprisoned three quarters of a mile in the depths of the earth, and the great unknown river shrinks into insignificance as it dashes its angry waves against the walls and cliffs that rise to the world above.

With some eagerness and some anxiety, we enter the canyon below and are carried along by the swift waters through walls which rise from its very edge. We run six miles in a little more than half an hour and emerge into a more open portion of the canyon. We stop to make a portage. Then on we go, stopping at a few points to examine rapids, which we find can be run, until we have made another five miles, when we land for dinner.

August 14—After breakfast we enter on the waves. The canyon is narrower than we have ever before seen it; the water is swifter; the walls are set with pinnacles and crags; and sharp, angular buttresses, which, bristling with wind- and wave-polished spires, extend far out into the river. As we proceed, the granite

RUNNING RAPIDS

rises higher, until nearly a thousand feet of the lower part of the walls are composed of this rock.

About 11 o'clock we hear a great roar ahead, and approach it very cautiously. The sound grows louder and louder as we run, and at last we find ourselves above a long, broken fall, with ledges and pinnacles of rock obstructing the river. There is a descent of perhaps 75 or 80 feet in a third of a mile, and the rushing waters break into great waves on the rocks, and lash themselves into a mad, white foam. A portage would be impractical, and we must run the rapids or abandon the river.

Running through Rapids

There is no hesitation. We step into our boats, push off, and away we go, first on smooth but swift water, then we strike a glassy wave and ride to its top, down again into the trough, up again on a higher wave, and down and up on waves higher and still higher until we strike one just as it curls back, and a breaker rolls over our little boat. Still onward we speed, shooting past projecting rocks, till the little boat is caught in a whirlpool and spun around several times. And now the other boats have passed us. Hurled back from a rock, now on this side, now on that, we are carried into an eddy, in which we struggle for a few minutes, and are then carried out again, the breakers still rolling over us. Our boat is unmanageable, and we drift another hundred yards through the breakers —how, we scarcely know. We find the other boats have turned into an eddy below the fall and are waiting to catch us as we come, for the men have seen that our boat is swamped.

Our boat bailed, on we go again. The walls are now more than a mile high. The gorge is black and narrow below, red and gray and flaring above, with crags and angular projections on the walls, which, cut in many places by side canyons, seem to be a vast wilderness of rocks. Down in these grand, gloomy depths we glide, ever listening, for the mad waters keep up their roar, ever watching, ever peering ahead, for the narrow canyon is winding and the river closed in so that we can see but a few hundred yards, and what there may be below we know not; so we listen for falls and watch for rocks, stopping now and then to admire the gigantic scenery.

August 15—The waters reel and roll and boil, and we are scarcely able to determine where we can go. The boats are entirely unmanageable; no order in their running can be preserved; now one, now another, is ahead, each crew laboring for its own preservation. It rains!

August 18—The day is employed in making portages and we advance but two miles. Still it rains.

August 19—Rain again this morning. We are in our granite prison still, and the time until noon is spent in making a long, bad portage.

August 20—The characteristics of the canyon change this morning. The river is broader, the walls more sloping, and composed of black slates

CLIMBING THE GRAND CANYON WALL

that stand on edge. We make 10 miles this afternoon.

August 25—Thirty-five miles today. Hurrah!

August 27—About 11 o'clock we come to a place in the river which seems much worse than any we have yet met in all its course. The afternoon is spent clambering among the crags and pinnacles and carefully scanning the river. We find that lateral streams have washed boulders into the river so as to form a dam, over which the water makes a broken fall of 18 or 20 feet; then there is a rapid, beset with rocks, for 200 or 300 yards. Below, there is a second fall; how great, we cannot tell.

The Group Splits Up

After supper Captain Howland asks to have a talk with me. We walk up the creek a short distance, and I soon find that his object is to remonstrate against my determination to proceed. He thinks that we had better abandon the river here. Talking with him, I learn that he, his brother and William Dunn have determined to go no farther in the boats.

August 28—After breakfast two rifles and a shotgun are given to the men who are going out. I ask them to help themselves to the rations and take what they think to be a fair share. This they refuse to do, saying they have no fear but that they can get something to eat.

Now we are all ready to start. The last thing before leaving, I write a letter to my wife and give it to Captain Howland. Sumner gives him his watch, directing that it be sent to his sister should he not be heard from again. The records of the expedition have been kept in duplicate. One of these sets is given to Howland.

Now we are ready, some tears are shed; it is a rather solemn parting; each party thinks the other is taking the dangerous course.

The three men climb a crag that overhangs the river to watch us off.

August 29—We start very early this morning. The river still continues swift, but we have no serious difficulty, and at 12 o'clock emerge from the Grand Canyon of the Colorado. We are in a valley now, and low mountains are seen rising in the distance, coming to the river below. We recognize this stream as the one called Grand Wash.

Tonight we camp on the left bank, in a mesquite thicket.

An End to Danger and Toil

The relief from danger and the joy of success are great. Every waking hour passed in the Grand Canyon has been one of toil. We have watched with deep solicitude the steady disappearance of our scant supply of rations, and from time to time have seen the river snatch a portion of the little left, while we were a-hungering. Only during the few hours of deep sleep has the roar of the waters been hushed. Now the danger is over, now the toil has ceased, now the gloom has disappeared, now the firmament is bounded only by the horizon, and what a vast expanse of constellations can be seen! The river rolls by us in silent majesty; the quiet of the camp is sweet; our joy is ecstasy. We sit till long after midnight talking of the Grand Canyon, talking of home.

POWELL'S MEN ON A HEIGHT ABOVE THE INNER GORGE

6/ The Challenge of White Water

Once in a lifetime, if one is lucky, one so merges with sunlight and air and running water that whole eons...might pass in a single afternoon without discomfort.

LOREN EISELEY/ *THE IMMENSE JOURNEY*

The early voyagers through the Grand Canyon, and even those who made the journey as late as the 1950s, were unusual men. It is not only that they had the courage to ride the then-uncontrolled river in small wooden boats. Most of them seem to have had other characteristics that set them apart—strength of body or mind and a general vigor or saltiness of personality uncommon in other men. The first to make the voyage, Major John Wesley Powell, whose journal of that trip has been excerpted on pages 120 through 129, was not exceptional simply because he had lost one arm; in the years following the Civil War there were thousands of ex-soldiers in similar condition. Powell was unusual because he combined a fine intellect with an occasional display of the quirkishness that often marks people of brilliance.

Powell had a close friend, an eminent geologist named W. J. McGee, who was a tall man. Powell himself was small. One day, while staring at McGee's head, Powell suddenly remarked, "I'll bet I have a bigger brain than you have."

McGee laughed but, observing that Powell was completely in earnest, accepted the bet. Each man would bequeath his brain to the other, and upon the death of the survivor, both brains would be delivered to a surgeon who would make comparative measurements. Powell died first, in 1902. His brain was immediately removed, placed in preserving fluid, and given to McGee. When McGee died in 1912 his brain was also removed and the measurements were duly made. Powell won the bet.

Among other unusual voyagers in the Grand Canyon were two small but muscular brothers named Ellsworth and Emery Kolb. In 1911, when many people scarcely knew what a movie was, the Kolb brothers not only ventured down the Colorado in wooden boats but took a heavy hand-cranked camera through the Canyon, making a motion picture as they went. Parts of it are still being shown two or three times a day to tourists in Grand Canyon village. Ellsworth Kolb died in 1960, but Emery Kolb, over 90, was still alive and alert when I talked to him in the early '70s. He came to the Grand Canyon in 1902, long before it was a national park, and has been there ever since, living in a house that overhangs the South Rim. Conversation with Mr. Kolb was baffling at first; sometimes he did not bother with antecedents in his conversation, a habit common to many elderly people, who take it for granted that their unspoken train of thought, their emotions and even their prejudices are shared by their listeners. Thus when I was introduced to Mr. Kolb, who was about five feet tall and whose long cheerful face reminded me of a grasshopper's, he looked straight at me and said, "Goddam Indian!"

For an instant I thought perhaps there was someone standing behind me. But the remark soon became clear. It seems that he had a storage bin with a heavy metal lid. He also had an Indian assistant. Mr. Kolb had recently been bending over, rummaging in the bin while his assistant held up the lid. Somehow the lid slipped and fell on the small of Mr. Kolb's back, injuring him enough so that he had to spend three days in a hospital. The whole question of Indian helpers, heavy metal lids and injuries still rankled in his bosom and he merely assumed that it rankled in mine as well. After a few minutes' talk I remarked that I, too, although in a far more modest and easier way, was going to make a voyage through the Canyon. "No one," he said sourly, "no one will ever know the Colorado as it really was. It's too late."

Mr. Kolb was right. Conditions have changed. When the gates of Glen Canyon Dam, near the northeastern end of the Grand Canyon, were closed for the first time in 1963, the Colorado was put under restraint. At times it can still behave with great ferocity but it is not the river that Powell or Kolb knew.

Nevertheless the Colorado remains one of the great rivers of America. From its source in the Rocky Mountains of Colorado, it runs 1,400 miles to the Gulf of California. But it no longer empties into the gulf, as it did for millions of years, because it is exhausted before it gets there.

What was formerly the mouth of the river is now merely a channel in which the tide of the sea ebbs and flows. So many cities, so many industries, so many huge agricultural enterprises have had a gulp of the Colorado that its last, lower reaches have become a desolation and a place of sand and mud. A whole river is being drunk up, indeed a whole river system, for all the hundreds of tributaries of the Colorado, among them the San Juan, the Green, the Gunnison, the Dirty Devil, the Yampa, the Gila and the Little Colorado, are being drunk up as well. This monstrous circumstance can be noted here only in passing. In the Grand Canyon section of the Colorado there is still plenty of water and that is the matter at hand.

The flow of water through the Grand Canyon depends largely on the amount that is released at Glen Canyon Dam. The dam is regarded with loathing by the members of the Sierra Club, the Friends of the Earth, and other conservationist groups and individuals, who believe it is wasteful, unnecessary and a monumental example of the harm that can be done when bureaucrats are seized with the compulsion to pour concrete. The dam has created a huge reservoir, Lake Powell, which has flooded one of the loveliest tracts of wilderness in North America. When he floated through Glen Canyon a century ago, Major Powell saw "royal arches, mossy alcoves, deep beautiful glens, and painted grottoes and a vast chamber, carved out of the rock. At the upper end there is a clear, deep pool of water, bordered with verdure. The chamber is more than 200 feet high, 500 feet long, and 200 feet wide. Through the ceiling, and on through the rocks for a thousand feet above, there is a narrow, winding skylight. Here we bring our camp. When my brother sings us a song at night, we are pleased to find that this hollow in the rock is filled with sweet sounds. It was doubtless made for an academy of music by its storm-born architect; so we name it Music Temple."

Lake Powell has drowned Music Temple and the rest of Glen Canyon. The water of the lake is backed up for about 180 miles into Utah, and is allowed to flow through the dam on a variable schedule related to the demand for power in such cities as Las Vegas, Phoenix and Tucson. And the demand in turn depends on the number of air conditioners, hair driers, television sets, electric can openers and electric guitars in use at the moment. Generally, between three and seven million gallons per minute flow through the dam, in contrast to the extremes of about half a million and 100 million in the pre-dam days of drought and flood, when the level of the river in Grand Canyon rose and fell with the seasons. In voyaging on the river today one can look up at the cliffs beside it and see driftwood, even large treetrunks, wedged years ago in the rock 60 or 70 feet overhead. At its present controlled and relatively low rate of flow, the river more or less maintains the level it had in the dry, late summers of the past century; it was in late summer of 1869 that Major Powell made his exploration of the Canyon. Thus the rapids now are much as they were then; it is possible to duplicate Powell's journey at least in that respect.

The dam has changed other aspects of the river in Grand Canyon. For one thing, the Colorado is not always *colorado*. Below the dam it is no longer red with silt but often appears pale green in the distance and glass clear up close. The silt, now trapped on the upstream side of the Glen Canyon Dam, settles in Lake Powell. In time the silt will fill the lake, as it has already begun to do, and the dam will become useless. Meanwhile the river below the dam will be clear, except when mud-bearing runoffs and floods come down the side canyons to redden it temporarily. The river will also be extremely cold the whole year round. In the generation of power, water is drawn from near the bottom of Lake Powell through penstocks, pipes 15 feet in diameter, and runs through turbines located about 600 feet below the top of the dam. The temperature of lake-bottom water remains around 50°. In summer it slowly warms as it flows through Grand Canyon, but even 100 miles below the dam it would still seem shockingly frigid to a man who found himself involuntarily swimming in it.

Its coldness is not the main reason why voyagers today approach the river with caution. In the 277-mile length of the Grand Canyon, the Colorado, which many white-water boatmen regard as the roughest navigable river in the world, drops 2,200 feet, with more than 150 rapids. Several of the rapids drop as much as 15 feet and one of them drops as much as 30. In some of the rapids the current is so savage that it can tear off a man's clothing, including belt, trousers and shoes. Alternating with the rapids there are long, deep pools where the gradient of the river is gentle, typically about three feet in a mile.

The river bed, even in the quiet pools, is extremely irregular. The water's depth may range from one foot or less to as much as 60 feet and back up to 20 feet in a distance of only a few hundred yards. The width varies from about 900 feet to as little as 50. These fluctuations in depth and width, combined with the steep gradient in the rapids, create powerful and strange formations among the rocks in the water. There are eddies with sharply defined shear zones—places where the current may be moving at five miles an hour in one direction while only two feet away it may be moving at five miles an hour the opposite way. Sometimes the river boils up in mounds or domes, as much as 40 feet across and three feet high in the center; at other times it forms vortexes or whirlpools six or seven feet deep.

Boatmen have long maneuvered through these startling water formations by instinct or trial and error, with little knowledge as to their cause. The first scientific study of them, *The Rapids and the Pools —Grand Canyon,* by Luna B. Leopold, a hydrologist with the U.S. Geological Survey, was published only in 1969. In investigating the whirlpools, Leopold on numerous occasions put fluorescein-dye markers into the water at the foot of large rapids. "The bag enclosing the dye was buoyant," he wrote, "for it was the type designed for the use of pilots shot down at sea. In several of these trials, the dye bag immediately disappeared and was dragged below the surface. . . . We circled in the pool for a considerable time, waiting to see where the dye marker would appear. In one instance it did not reach the surface again until it had been taken downstream nearly a quarter of a mile."

Dr. Leopold's paper is an unusual piece of prose to be published by the government. Like Lieutenant Ives reporting on his efforts in the 1850s to take the steamboat *Explorer* from the mouth of the Colorado to the head of navigation, Leopold was emotionally moved by the Canyon and the river. He began his study in words that are a long way removed from bureaucratic jargon:

"In the dry glare of a sun-drenched afternoon, in the bitter chill of a thunderstorm wind, or in the purple evening, there is no respite from the incessant boom of the great river. One finds at times he has forgotten the ever-present roar of the rapids and then, as if suddenly awakened, he hears it again. So persistent is the sound that I often wonder how the mind can put away the noise into some recess, even momentarily.

"The river's boom is associated with a pervasive uneasiness which never leaves a man while he is clamped within the cliffs of the canyon. This uneasiness is not the reflection of a queasy stomach for, in fact, the dry air, the sun-dappled water, and the intense color tend to give a sense of exhilaration. Rather, the uneasiness is a subdued but undeniable cold fear which never departs."

Dr. Leopold's opening remarks seem to constitute both a salute to the river and a warning. A leisurely journey down the Colorado through the Grand Canyon is one of the loveliest journeys a man may take, but he should bear in mind that the Canyon, like any wilderness, can kill as easily as it captivates. It can drown him or split him on a rock or drop a boulder on him. It can imprison and starve him. It can cause him to become lost so that—never far from all that water—he dies of thirst or fries to death in the sun. The river and the Canyon frequently kill people —about a half dozen every year—but as a rule the victims are the sort who might otherwise be killed jaywalking, speeding or drinking the contents of a bottle without reading the label; the wilderness does not often kill people who have a decent respect for it.

One such senseless death occurred recently when a young man encountered the sacred datura, a hallucinogenic plant that grows in the bottom of the Grand Canyon and in many parts of the West. Its biological name is *Datura meteloides,* and various Indian tribes once used it in their religious ceremonies to induce dreams and visions. Under the influence of the potent datura, the young man decided he could swim the Colorado. His body was recovered five weeks later.

Martin Litton, the man with whom I was to voyage through the Canyon, is as unusual in his own way as Major Powell, the Kolb brothers and all the others who have run the rapids in little wooden boats. His uniqueness, however, is not immediately apparent. It is only after a few encounters with him that a man can begin to savor Litton's character: he is an American original, independent, brave and as tough-minded as they come. He is a director of the Sierra Club, but was deeply concerned about the fate of the earth long before such words as ecology and environmentalist became fashionable. The thought of Glen Canyon Dam and the harm it is doing to the once-mighty Colorado causes Litton to grind his teeth. "The increasing generation of power, much of it for unnecessary purposes, will soon wipe out what's left of nature. In fact it will wipe out people too."

Litton first went through the Canyon, solely for adventure, in 1955. At that time the Glen Canyon Dam had not been built, the river was still as formidable as Powell had found it, and running the rapids was regarded as a hazardous and noteworthy deed—so noteworthy, in fact, that even at that late date historians were still keeping count of the people who had done it. Counting Powell and all his crew, counting the Kolb brothers, parties of government surveyors and all other bold souls who had made the voyage since 1869, Litton was the 185th. That may seem a high number, but in view of the time lapse of 86 years since Powell's first journey, it is in fact quite a low number.

In recent years Litton has been operating a small, part-time business called Grand Canyon Dories. He owns several specially built rowboats, which are descendants of the old Grand Banks fishing dories that once skimmed over heavy seas far out in the North Atlantic. The boats have remarkable rough-water capability, and in them Litton takes passengers through the Canyon on voyages that last about three weeks. By the early '70s he had taken some 300 people through, bringing the total number who had made the journey in small wooden boats to about 500.

There are other ways of going, however. Many people—perhaps 30,000—have made the trip in big, military-surplus neoprene pontoons powered by outboard motors. The tautly inflated pontoons, run by some 20 commercial companies also licensed by the Park Service, are called baloney boats by those who regard that manner of travel as too easy, like mountain climbing with the aid of a helicopter. Litton himself has misgivings about the volume of traffic now plying the river. "The only way we can save any wilderness in this country," he says, "is to make it harder to get into, and harder to stay in once you get there."

The motorized pontoons do indeed have certain drawbacks. They make the Canyon trip in from eight to 10 days, too quickly for the voyagers to become intimately acquainted with the river. They are crowded; some of them carry as many as 30 passengers wearing bulky orange life jackets. And the exhaust fumes and the smell of raw gasoline are at odds with nature. One man who had made such a voyage, riding in the second pontoon in a convoy of three, told me unhappily that he imagined he could taste gasoline in everything he ate and drank for several days afterward, and that for a while even his wife smelled to him like an Esso station.

Litton's rowboats are not much larger than the craft that can be rented on lakes in municipal parks. They can comfortably accommodate an oarsman and four passengers, and as a rule the boats travel through the Canyon in groups of four to six. Because of their special broad-beamed, double-ended design they are no more hazardous to ride in than the pontoon boats. None of Litton's passengers has drowned or been seriously injured. The dories, like the big pontoons, occasionally flip upside down in the rapids and the passengers get wet, cold and scared. They are buoyed by their life jackets, and when they are dry, warm and calm again they look back on the wild adventure and are glad it happened.

I had arranged to meet Martin Litton in mid-June at Lee's Ferry in northern Arizona, near the Utah border, where the Grand Canyon begins. While hiking along the rims and inside the Canyon I had seen the

Colorado a good many times but had thought of it mainly in remote, geological terms: what it had done to the Canyon in the past 10 million years or might do in another 10 million. Now I began to wonder what it might do in the next few weeks. Very early one morning I went out to Moran Point on the South Rim. From there I could see Hance Rapids in the river far below, little flecks of white in a streak of water that appeared no more than half an inch wide. Hance is generally acknowledged to be one of the toughest rapids in the Grand Canyon. I held my breath in the quietness, listened and could hear the distant, seashell sound of it a full three miles away.

When I joined Martin Litton's party he was unloading his dories from small trailers with the help of a half dozen boatmen. Litton is a big man, over six feet and weighing 210 pounds, with a pleasant face and a relaxed, shockproof manner. He earns no money from his directorship in the Sierra Club and makes his living as a journalist and photographer. But his heart is in the wilderness or he would never have gone into the dory business. He had just completed the first of four voyages he intended to make during the summer. He rows through the Canyon and is met at the end, on Lake Mead, by a motorboat that tows him down the lake to Temple Bar, where he hauls out his boats and takes them 300 miles overland to Lee's Ferry to begin the next trip.

One of the dories was already in the water. In large gold letters on the bow, legible at about 100 yards, were the words *Music Temple*. Litton names all of his boats in memory of natural wonders that have been obliterated or defaced. On a trailer nearby was the *Diamond Head,* which commemorates what used to be one of the most spectacular sights on earth, the view of Diamond Head from Waikiki Beach in Hawaii—now destroyed by a screen of high-rise apartment buildings and hotels. Litton's own boat, the *Diablo Canyon,* is named for what was one of the last large pieces of seaside wilderness in California until a huge nuclear power plant began to rise there.

The *Music Temple* was only 16 feet long but unusually broad in the beam, nearly seven feet, and flat bottomed. Both its bow and its tapered stern had a pronounced upward rake; the boat could go through rough water with either end foremost. It was made of marine plywood attached to a stout frame and had a watertight compartment in the bow, another in the stern and several others around the cockpit where the oarsman and passengers sat. All of these could be opened to receive stores of food and the rubberized bags in which most of the 24 passengers had packed their gear. Several of the passengers had come from states as far away as Florida and Washington, Louisiana and Connecticut. There was a girl of 14, with her parents, and two couples who were past 60, although the average age appeared to be about 30.

It was 5 o'clock in the afternoon when all six dories were finally in the water, loaded and ready to move. The passengers got aboard and the boats glided out into midstream and started down the river. Litton rowed the first boat; the other oarsmen were young men in their twenties whom he had trained. Some were college graduates, others were dropouts. There were beards, one large drooping mustache and an assortment of hair styles. One man of 25, who stood six feet four in his bare feet, wore a single gold earring as well as a full beard. His long hair was tied by a thong at the nape of his neck. He had formidable muscles and the Canyon sun had tanned him the color of old leather. The impression he created was that of a boatswain or gunner's mate from an 18th Century ship of the line. Another young oarsman, clean shaven and crew cut, was a schoolteacher. A third, whose hair fell almost to his shoulders, was the son of a Hollywood film producer, while a fourth, with medium-length hair and a beard like General Grant's, had recently earned an advanced degree in geology.

The river at Lee's Ferry was calm, with a current of only three or four miles an hour. Here, between the deep gorges of Glen Canyon to the northeast and Grand Canyon to the southwest, the Colorado runs briefly through fairly open country. A small tributary stream, the Paria, enters the Colorado near Lee's Ferry and it is from this point that all mileage in the Grand Canyon is measured. When, for example, the hydrologist Luna Leopold writes that the maximum depth he has found in the river is 110 feet at mile 114.3, he is referring to a point exactly that distance from Lee's Ferry.

Immediately below Lee's Ferry the cliffs began to rise on both sides of the river. Like a series of colossal wedges sliding beneath each other, the rock strata that form the Canyon walls appeared, one by one: the cream-colored Kaibab Limestone, the buff Toroweap Limestone, the white Coconino Sandstone, then the red and maroon Hermit Shale followed by the red Supai Sandstone and the Redwall Limestone. As each formation emerged at water level, seeming to push the other formations upward, the cliffs increased in height and soon they towered 2,000 feet overhead. Over the ages the Redwall has been so smoothly polished by the river that it reminded Major Powell of marble. To this

Gracefully curving their slender branches, tamarisks crowd the beaches of the Colorado River near the entrance to Whitmore Canyon.

day the long, narrow gorge below Lee's Ferry, though part of the Grand Canyon, is called Marble Canyon.

Litton rowed quietly. He continually glanced at his dories to see how they were riding, to make sure the weight was properly distributed and to size up the passengers: how were they reacting with 50 feet of cold water beneath them? The passengers presumably would not have been present if they were afraid of water but even those who were widely traveled and had seen many kinds of water around the world had not yet seen the kind that lay ahead of them. Litton looked to see whether, by some unlucky chance, he was carrying someone likely to panic. He studied the sky, the current and the water level, trying to calculate how many feet or inches of clearance there might be over various rocks of his acquaintance in Badger Creek Rapids. The rapids were now close at hand, at mile 7.8.

Boatmen in North America have adopted a scale for rating rapids that like the Richter scale, which measures earthquakes, classifies them according to their violence. It runs from 1 to 10. Anything above 10—and there is at least one such rapids in Grand Canyon—is classed as "not recommended," which means that it is the mother of catastrophes. A No. 1 rapids is called a riffle; 2 and 3 are light; 4, 5 and 6 are medium; 7, 8 and 9 are heavy; and 10 is the maximum recommended, even for the most experienced river runners in the best of boats.

Badger Creek Rapids is a fair introduction to white water. It has a rating of 7 and drops 15 feet. It contains boulders 15 feet in diameter and makes a low growling sound that can be heard half a mile away. Along the smooth pool at its head there are sandbanks on which grow clumps of willow and tamarisk. The latter is an exotic, feathery tree native to the eastern Mediterranean. Covered with small pink flowers in the spring, this handsome tree was imported into California as a windbreak at the turn of the century and since that time has been spreading vigorously along Western streams and rivers; now it can be found as far as 1,000 miles from the Pacific coast and it is still spreading.

"How tough a rapids is Badger?" Litton was asked.

"Terrifying," he said with a faint smile. "Powell carried his boats around it." However, Litton's six dories boomed through in about 30 seconds, not enough time for the passengers to become much alarmed, merely overconfident. Litton continued to smile at no one in particular.

The boats pulled ashore for the night just below the rapids. There are none too many riverside campsites, at least for groups as large as

30, in the Canyon. For miles the walls plunge directly into the river; elsewhere the narrow ledges and talus slopes along the water's edge are too rugged to permit many people to lie down; and in other places a shelf of sand, comfortably above water level at dusk, may be a foot submerged by dawn. During his exploration of the river a century ago Powell often had difficulty in finding good sites, and apparently was so little interested in creature comforts that he did not try very hard. In Lodore Canyon, some distance upstream, one of Powell's boatmen wrote bitterly in his diary that Powell had exercised his usual bad taste in locating a camp, adding that, "If I had a dog that would lie down where my bed is made tonight, I would kill him and burn his collar and swear I never owned him."

Litton showed better taste. The camp below Badger Creek, on a boulder-strewn sandy beach, had ample space and a good supply of dry driftwood for the fire. It was fairly close to the rapids, however, and I supposed the sound might make it difficult to sleep. I lay down at nightfall, looking up at the sky, listening in awe to one of the most powerful and complex natural sounds on earth. Although it is commonplace to say that big rapids sound like a freight train, it is true. Freight trains make many sounds at once and so do rapids. The roar is not steady but pulsating, alive and sometimes, unaccountably, there comes out of the water an iron groan like that of a train on a curve. Like the sound of wheels on track joints, there is a continual faint clicking of cobblestones ricocheting off boulders. There are clanks, poundings and tremendous hissings and seethings.

But, surprisingly, the noise of rapids is also lulling, and when full darkness finally descended into Marble Canyon the whole camp had fallen asleep, seemingly unworried about what the Colorado River might do to them in the morning.

7/ Riding the Rapids

*We had learned to discriminate by its noise, long before
we could see a rapid, whether it was filled with rocks,
or was merely a descent of big water. The latter, often just as
impressive as the former, had a sullen, steady boom; the
rocky rapids had the same sound, punctuated by
another sound, like the crack of regiments of musketry.*

ELLSWORTH KOLB/ *THROUGH THE GRAND CANYON FROM WYOMING TO MEXICO*

As dawn drifted down into the camp below Badger Creek Rapids, waking the voyagers there, the soft sand by the river appeared printed with innumerable tracks that had not been seen at nightfall: rows of paired quotation marks, parallel columns of dashes, asterisks, commas, periods —all the punctuation necessary for a thesis on life in the Sonoran Zones. In the glare of noon it had seemed that few creatures could live in the hot gorges of the Canyon; but daybreak revealed the contrary.

Most of the small animals that make their home on or near the Canyon bottom are nocturnal. In the furnace blast of the day they doze in shaded crevices, but at night, when the boulders and rock walls are still radiating enough solar heat to keep the air temperature at 80° or even 90°, they come out to hunt and to eat. Along the river's edge were the footprints of a little spotted skunk, the smallest of its kind in the United States. It is not much larger than a squirrel, black, with white pencil stripes on its back and polka dots scattered from its nose to its plumed tail. There were the tracks of pocket mice and kangaroo rats and the ring-tailed cacomistle; of insects, lizards and scorpions. Most of the lizards can stand great heat and may be seen even in daytime. As they scurry along the sand they drag their long, thin tails, leaving trails that suggest the wakes of tiny four-oared racing shells.

The deep gorges are by no means teeming with life, however. A man must wander all around the camp with his eyes fixed on the sand to find where the hunters and promenaders and scouts of the night have passed; yet the life is there. But just as we were becoming absorbed in the search for new tracks, the river reasserted itself with a roar.

Martin Litton was already walking on the shore examining the sky, the cliffs, the water and the general state of the Canyon. Litton, as a United States citizen, is part owner of the Grand Canyon and all other undeveloped public lands and takes his ownership seriously. He has been defending the wilderness all his adult life. Twenty years ago, when he was a feature writer for the *Los Angeles Times*, his was a lonely voice crying in, or at least about, the wilderness. "When the people of the United States," he wrote, "discover what they own in these unscarred, unsurpassed, unbelievable wilderness areas, they will never surrender them up for materialist uses."

At breakfast Litton spoke with mock dread of the rapids at Soap Creek, a few miles downstream. As he had done with Badger Creek Rapids, he described it as horrifying and awful. His method worked, and by the time the boats had slipped out into the river no one seemed in the least apprehensive. Soap Creek Rapids, however, is not a gentle stretch of water. It has a rating of 8, heavy, and a fall of 17 feet.

Soap Creek has dug a deep side canyon that enters the Grand Canyon from the west. Sometimes the side canyon is dry or merely damp, but a few times in a century flash floods thunder down it. These gully washers carry not only sand, gravel and cobbles but boulders as large as houses. The debris is spewed out of the mouth of the side canyon into the channel of the Colorado, creating a partial dam that in turn creates a rapids with a long, quiet pool above. Most of the other rapids in the Grand Canyon have been made in this same manner.

As we floated through the pool above Soap Creek I looked toward the rapids and was startled to see that down where the rumbling and roaring were at their loudest, the river dropped out of sight. From one bank to the other there was a flat sheet of water but beyond that, nothing. Such a sight is stimulating to the curiosity, and I began to stare at the place where the river vanished. As we drew closer to it, there became visible beyond the drop-off scattered rooster tails and haystacks

•

of water flying into the air. I was riding in Litton's boat and turned to look at him. He shrugged and said, "Terrifying."

In running big rapids, whether in a small rowboat or a big rubber pontoon, the tactic is to slide down the tongue. The tongue is a V-shaped chute of smooth water, the narrow end pointing downstream, which contains no waves, whirlpools, rocks or other obstructions. The tongue need not be located in midstream; it may be anywhere between the banks; but wherever it is, the tongue is the place to enter rapids. If it should chance that there is no tongue, no place where a boat may get a reasonable start into the rapids, three choices are open. The first is to burn the boat, swear you never owned it, and climb out of the Canyon —if you can. The second is to carry the boat around the rapids and put it back in the water downstream—if you can. The third is to line the boat: by means of long ropes attached to bow and stern and handled by strong and skillful men clambering along the rocks on the shore, the empty craft may be maneuvered downstream. Litton sometimes lines or portages his boats, but on this trip he did neither. He ran all the rapids. Before he attempted this one, however, he wanted to look it over carefully. The current in the pool at the head of the rapids was not strong. The boatmen had no difficulty in pulling to the shore. Litton got out; the boatmen got out; and all the passengers got out too.

After studying the rapids for a few minutes Litton decided on the course that seemed most likely to take him past the worst of the holes and rocks. We returned to the boats, tightened the fastenings on our life jackets and started in slow column formation toward the rapids. Litton went first, occasionally standing up in his boat to make certain that he was headed directly for the tongue. It may seem contrary to the principles of good seamanship to stand up in a boat at any time, least of all while approaching a boiling cauldron of white water, but all experienced rivermen do it. Conventional seamanship also calls for an oarsman to face backward while he moves forward, occasionally glancing over his shoulder to check his course. However, Colorado boatmen have long since learned to turn their craft around before entering rapids and face forward, in the direction they are going, and row with the current. They can see what lies ahead of them and can control the boats more easily. The unusual design of Litton's dories now appeared admirable: their tapered, peaked sterns would serve equally well as bows, and their exceptionally broad flat bottoms and high flared sides would presumably prevent them from turning over.

At the beginning of the tongue, the water was dark and moving with great power, smooth and ominously gentle. It gripped the boat and began to sweep it down a polished slope toward the maelstrom at the bottom where the rapids exploded. Waves, a few of them 10 feet from trough to crest, rushed heaving and hissing at the boat. The peaked stern served its purpose well; the dory rose to meet the waves without burying itself in them. In the middle of the rapids the boat was plunging along at about 20 miles an hour—a modest pace, to be sure, although there is another way of looking at it. The dory was 16 feet long and it was moving at two boat's lengths per second. At that speed, if the boat should be bearing down on a rock 100 feet away, there would be only about three seconds to make adjustments. To keep his craft on a safe course, Litton at times literally bent the oars, which are made of top-grade ash, the wood commonly used for baseball bats.

Partway through the rapids he skirted a deep hole, beyond which loomed an extraordinary object that appeared to be a sculpture in water. It had raised itself several feet out of the river, it was certainly liquid, yet it did not move. Such things are described in the literature of rivers and in textbooks about hydraulics, where they seem credible. It is only when a man actually looks at one that he doubts it.

This fluid sculpture is called a standing wave; and it is a fair description: a wave that stands still while the river flows through it. This one was of modest height, about 12 feet. There are others in the Colorado that rise twice that high. Standing waves are created by obstructions in the river bed. When there is an extremely large rock in rapids the water must flow over or around it. Immediately downstream from the rock the water accelerates, its added speed creating turbulence that forces it down to form a hole. Sometimes the hole is so deep that even one of the big rubber baloney boats may be lost from sight in it. Just below the hole the water rears up in an apparently motionless wave with a crest that curls upstream.

There are other surprising waves in the rapids of the Colorado. When the channel narrows, water is forced from the sides toward the center. Thus at times there may be a wild pile-up in which the waves come at a boat from the left, right or both at once in a herringbone pattern. Or perhaps the boat will careen for a moment along a pressure ridge in midriver and then slide off to one side. At the foot of large rapids the water, guided by the lay of the rocks, is often thrown against one bank. If the bank is on a curve and consists of a vertical cliff, the water rebounds to form a powerful eddy or reverse current on the opposite side

A still pool at the entrance to Redwall Cavern mirrors the towering cliffs and the fleecy clouds of an afternoon sky.

of the river; and if a boat is caught on the line where the opposing currents adjoin, it can be spun around with surprising speed.

A moment after passing the standing wave Litton's boat was assaulted by a wave of a different sort against which its special design was powerless. The wave leaped over the stern (now serving as the bow) where I was sitting and for a moment it buried me. It was light blue green and very cold. It was also very fast, like a good boxer. It did not have the ponderous, wrestling approach of ocean surf but instead it threw one quick, solid punch. Then with a thud it collapsed in the boat, filling it to the gunwales. The watertight compartments kept the boat from sinking, but it was swamped. We were sitting waist deep in the Colorado, still booming along past the rocks and holes. I glanced at Litton again and this time he was not smiling. He was grinning. "Horrible," he said, bending the oars as he altered course.

Immediately beside me sat a small, slender lady, Mrs. Richard A. Sanders of Decatur, Georgia, who was riding through the Grand Canyon on vacation with her husband. She was wearing a large old-fashioned white sunbonnet neatly tied under her chin and she was 63 years old. That wave punched Mrs. Sanders just as suddenly as it hit me. "Well," was all she said, and then she picked up a bailing bucket and in a brisk, housewifely manner started to remove the river from the boat. By the time we reached calm water below Soap Creek Rapids the Colorado had been put back in its place.

As we went deeper into the Canyon, running through rapids every two or three miles, it became routine for waves to jump into the boat and to be tossed out again in buckets. Sometimes the water in the boat was ankle deep, sometimes knee deep, but it seemed unlikely that we would sink unless the boat were demolished on a boulder. Rarely, one of the dories would strike a rock half hidden in the white water and it would be necessary to pull ashore and make repairs. Dispersed in the compartments of the small fleet was an assortment of sheathing and bracing, calking and carpenter's tools. The appearance of the lean boatmen, shaping and fitting patches to their dories beneath the many-colored cliffs, suggested New England fishermen who had taken a wrong turn somewhere and gotten as lost as it is possible for sailors to get.

Riders in the baloney boats get drenched as often as those in the dories. The standard rig consists of two banana-shaped pontoons about four feet in diameter and 10 yards long with a rubber barge lashed between them. The craft undulate and sometimes jackknife in the rapids;

water cascades over them. When the rubber is cut by rocks, the outboard-motor operators sew it up, making the seam waterproof with contact adhesive. And large though they are, the baloney boats, like the dories, can be savagely tossed and smashed by the Colorado. In 1967 one of the motorized pontoon boats was thrown upside down in major rapids and the motorman, entangled in some lines, was trapped beneath it and drowned. None of the passengers was hurt.

In memory of the late boatman his friends attached an inscribed aluminum pot lid to a rock beside the water at mile 150, where the drowning had occurred. There are other points where survivors have left markers for their dead companions. One of these is just below Soap Creek Rapids. Litton points it out, not as a grim curiosity but perhaps because he finds poetic justice in it. In this case the drowned man fully intended to tamper with the Canyon, and he was killed trying.

The inscription, chipped into red sandstone a few feet above normal waterline, reads: "F. M. Brown Pres. D.C.C. & P.R.R. Co., was drowned July 10, 1889, opposite this point." The initials are those of the Denver, Colorado Canyon and Pacific Railroad Company, of which Frank M. Brown was president. It was 20 years after Powell's voyage of exploration before anyone figured out how the Canyon might be put to materialist use, but Brown finally did it. There were great supplies of coal in Colorado, he noted, but none on the West Coast. To get the coal to California it had to be carried by rail over high mountains, an expensive operation. Brown knew that "water level" rail routes in the East had saved their builders millions by following river valleys that cut through mountain barriers or avoided them altogether.

Brown proposed building a railroad from Colorado to San Diego by way of the Grand Canyon and other canyons upstream, including Cataract, Glen and Marble. Brown calculated that because the road would not have to be built over mountains he could deliver coal in San Diego at about half the going rate and still make a fortune. Accordingly he set out with a surveying party to determine exactly where he would place his line. The group set off in six little boats made of brittle cedar, each 15 feet long, only three feet wide and weighing 150 pounds. He thought life preservers were needless encumbrances, though at least one of his companions begged him to invest in cork jackets. The river, Brown figured, would not dare to drown the president of the D.C.C. & P.R.R. Co. A few miles into the Canyon, Brown's boat capsized and he did drown. When his companions came up to the place where his boat had overturned, all they could find was his notebook circling in a whirlpool. His body was never recovered. The inscription was chipped into the rock and the expedition continued, headed now by Robert Stanton, chief engineer of the proposed railroad.

Thirteen miles farther down the Canyon the river swallowed a second boat, taking two men with it. Stanton decided to postpone the survey for a few months and resume it with better boats and equipment, including life preservers. He cached his supplies in a cave (still known as Stanton's Cave) about 100 feet above the river level at mile 31.4, and climbed up to the plateau with his surviving men. In December of 1889 Stanton returned and completed the survey all the way to the Gulf of California. He found the route feasible, though a bridge and several tunnels would have to be built and countless tons of explosives used to blast the heart out of the riverside cliffs. However, Stanton could not raise enough capital, and the project was abandoned.

Though Stanton may not have known it, his supplies shared the cave with some curious objects that have attracted the attention of Southwestern archeologists: wooden figurines that apparently represent bighorn sheep, antelope and deer. Found in several caves, the figurines are all constructed of split willow twigs in the same basic pattern, and many of them are pierced by miniature spears made of small sticks or thorns. They do not resemble any religious objects or toys belonging to Indians of historic times, nor is there any indication that their makers, whoever they may have been, lived in the caves. Apparently they merely paused there, left the figurines and departed. The best guess is that the little split-twig animals were used in rituals by nomadic hunters —perhaps if a symbolic deer were killed by a symbolic spear, the hunters might have good luck in reality. In 1963 one of the figurines from Stanton's Cave was radiocarbon-tested to determine its age. It turned out to be 4,000 years old. No evidence of earlier human life has yet been found in the Grand Canyon, although Indians were living in other parts of the Southwest as long as 25,000 years ago.

However, there are scores of stone dwellings and granaries of later Indians tucked in the crannies and side canyons, and many of them can be reached from the river. Since Litton's journeys down the Colorado are unhurried (he averages only about four hours a day on the river and on some days he does not travel at all) there is plenty of time to look at Indian ruins. Most of the ruins are the work of Pueblo Indians who came into the Canyon around 1000 A.D., but vanished, for unknown reasons, before the arrival of the Spaniards.

Not far downriver from Stanton's Cave Litton's party encountered an astonishing sight where the Colorado makes a sharp turn to the east. It was a view that delighted Powell when he saw it: "The river . . . seems enclosed by a wall set with a million brilliant gems. . . . On coming nearer we find fountains bursting from the rock high overhead, and the spray in the sunshine forms the gems which bedeck the wall. The rocks below the fountain are covered with mosses and ferns and many beautiful flowering plants." Powell named the place Vasey's Paradise, in honor of his friend Dr. George Vasey, a botanist in the U.S. Department of Agriculture. Having worked its way down through many layers of rocks, the water of the fountains emerges at a highly variable rate that depends on the amount of rainfall; often the water makes little more than broad sprinkles on the cliff, but occasionally it gushes at 4,000 gallons a minute, creating a green garden on the slope above the river. The greenery seems particularly handsome because the Canyon walls from Lee's Ferry to this point at mile 31.9 are almost bare, with only scattered clumps of prickly pear and other spiny plants growing in windowboxlike niches where a few handfuls of soil provide rootholds.

The gorge of the Colorado at Vasey's Paradise is about 2,500 feet in depth, and as boats descend through the rapids and the pools it grows deeper at the rate of 50 feet a mile. Down the straight reaches of the river or up through the gates of the side canyons, one can see towering walls and buttes glowing in hues of gold and rust, and sometimes in the far distance there is a glimpse of the high, cool rim of the Kaibab Plateau green with pines. Close at hand the Redwall Limestone has finally raised the last of its 500-foot cliffs out of the river and the gray-green Muav Limestone appears beneath it. The Redwall is not uniform in color at this level, as it will be farther downstream when it is far overhead and uniformly stained. Here it is brownish at its base, ribboned in light to dark gray in its middle elevations; higher still its layered beds are candy-striped in carmine, gray and brown. In several places the lower Redwall contains beds of the bright red quartz called jasper, some of it of semiprecious quality. There are numerous caves in the Redwall, made by the percolation of water through the limestone. Many of them are high in the cliffs where they occasionally occur in pairs, suggesting the eyes of death's-heads or of enormous owls.

One of the largest caves is just above water level at a bend in the river near mile 33. It is shaped like a band shell about 300 feet wide and 150 deep, with a vaulted ceiling that is perhaps 100 feet high at its midpoint. The floor is of smooth, whitish sand, sloping gently upward from the water's edge to the rear wall. Powell made camp here a century ago, describing the cavern as "a vast half-circular chamber which, if utilized for a theatre, would give seating to 50,000 people."

It is difficult to put aside thoughts of the one-armed Major Powell while running the river, particularly during the approach to heavy rapids. He made the ultimate bet, his life, on the chance that the Colorado contained no waterfalls, no sheer drops over which his boats would be swept. It was an informed bet. As a student of geology Powell assumed that a river with the rasping, cutting power of the Colorado would be unlikely to have vertical ledges in its channel; it would grind them down into rapids that, however fearsome, could still be passed.

But this was only an assumption and there were times when Powell had the gravest doubts about it. On August 10, 1869, after he had spent five days making his way down from Lee's Ferry through the Marble Gorge section of the Grand Canyon, he reached the confluence of the Colorado and the Little Colorado, at mile 61, and camped there for three nights before pushing on. In Major Powell's account there is a dramatic passage, written on the last night at the Little Colorado camp, that has been read by almost every voyager who has followed him: "August 13. We are now ready to start on our way down the Great Unknown. . . . We have but a month's rations remaining. The flour has been re-sifted through the mosquito-net sieve; the spoiled bacon has been dried and the worst of it boiled; the few pounds of dried apples have been spread in the sun and reshrunken to their normal bulk; the sugar has all melted and gone on its way down the river. . . .

"We have an unknown distance yet to run; an unknown river yet to explore. What falls there are, we know not; what rocks beset the channel, we know not; what walls rise over the river, we know not. Ah, well! we may conjecture many things. The men talk as cheerfully as ever; jests are bandied about freely this morning; but to me the cheer is somber and the jests are ghastly."

Martin Litton sometimes quotes parts of Powell's passage in a hollow voice as his boats approach a very tough section of the Colorado that begins at mile 72. Powell reached this section only a day after experiencing his time of doubt, and the river did its best to justify his fears. In nine miles there are five rapids: Unkar, Seventy-five Mile, Hance, Sockdolager and Grapevine; they drop 25, 15, 30, 19 and 18 feet respectively—Niagara Falls on the installment plan. Three of the rapids, depending on the level of the river, are in the "maximum recommended" category. The section where a new layer of stone called Shinumo Quartzite emerges from the river is made to seem even more formidable by an optical illusion. Instead of lying parallel with the water surface, the layer is tilted in such a way that when a man glances at the sloping lines of the quartzite in the walls of the gorge, the gradient of the river is exaggerated by an angle of about 15 degrees, and he has the alarming impression that his boat is rushing downstream much faster than it really is.

Powell had a good deal of trouble with the five heavy rapids, but got through with no casualties. So did Litton. However, as the river pounded and tossed the dories it was apparent that, although they were unsinkable, some of them were going to be flipped upside down; if not today, then tomorrow, or if not tomorrow, soon. The Colorado was too tough and too unpredictable to permit all the boats to go through the Canyon unscathed. Litton and his boatmen had survived several upsets on earlier voyages—the life jackets worn are big, wrap-around vests with high collars, buoyant enough to keep a swimmer afloat even in a whirlpool. Thus the thought of being thrown into the thundering white water was one that a man could live with. To be sure, a man could live even better without it, but the river would not let him put it out of his mind. Neither would the passengers in the big pontoons that came buzzing and smoking past from time to time. They would stare incredulously at the sight of the small wooden boats, take pictures, and then one of them would shout, "You've *got* to be kidding."

Near mile 77, in the midst of the five tough rapids, the river enters a forbidding, narrow V-shaped corridor named Upper Granite Gorge. Powell's men found it depressing—its crags and buttresses have a gray, Gothic look and the stone in the lower walls is very dark, almost black. This is the nethermost of all stones in the Canyon, the two-billion-year-old Vishnu Schist. When one at last comes face to face with it, after reading about it in geology handbooks or standing on the rim trying to catch a glimpse of it, the sight is strangely chilling. In its darkness and hardness there is preserved no trace of life of any kind, not the smallest fossil fragment to suggest that living things had ever existed or might ever exist. For an instant a voyager is filled with a sense of unspeakable loneliness and sadness.

The black schist forms the walls of the Inner Gorge of the Canyon for many miles, although it is often broken by seams of pink granite, and there are areas where subsidence and folding of the earth have brought the overlying sandstone and limestone down again to the river's edge. The gorge never closes in to claustrophobic narrowness, but there are long stretches of it that are impossible to enter or leave except by boat. In a few places human skeletons or remains, mummified by the dry air, have been found; presumably they are what is left of prospectors who came downriver on rafts or boats, cracked up in the rapids, and were unable to climb out. In 1906 one skeleton was found partway up the wall of the gorge near mile 90. It was still clothed, and in its pockets there were some crisp copies of Los Angeles newspapers dated 1900.

The dryness of the air in the Canyon, even within a few feet of the river, has some interesting effects on live humans as well as dead ones. Unlike hikers, who must carry water with them, river runners need only scoop up as much of the Colorado as they want. The river has not yet been as dangerously polluted as other watersheds, but to be on the safe side the National Park Service recommends that its water be purified before drinking.

As a rule people on the river drink all the water they require, but sometimes they do not and become dangerously dehydrated without realizing it. The loss of moisture through breathing and perspiration is so fast and so extreme in the heat of the Canyon that its extent may not be noticed, particularly since perspiration dries instantly on emerging from the skin. The effects can be felt mentally as well as physically. On a recent trip through the Canyon, Litton carried a middle-aged lady who turned to her companions, after a silence, and abruptly said, "What am I doing in this boat?" This was taken as a joke; after shooting a couple of ferocious rapids, people sometimes wonder what they are doing in boats in the Canyon. And presently she said, "Why am I wearing this ridiculous hat?" which was also regarded as mildly funny; the broad-brimmed hats worn to prevent sunburn sometimes have an odd look. But when she persisted in asking questions it became plain that she really had no idea where she was, or indeed who. Dehydration had temporarily blocked out her memory. The next day, with plenty of water plus a spoonful of mineral diet supplement, she recovered.

All things considered, the bottom of the Grand Canyon is a very poor place in which to become ill or to have an accident. Radio transmitters carried a mile deep in a stone gorge are not very effective in summoning help; the signals can scarcely be detected up on the rim. The chances are slim that distress markers placed on the riverbank will be noticed by planes flying far overhead. In the 277-mile length of the Canyon there is only one place—Diamond Creek at mile 226—where rescue vehicles can reach the river, over a rugged road that follows a stream down from the South Rim.

The possibility of injury in the Canyon is therefore bound at least to cross the mind of everyone who ventures down the Colorado. It also occurs to the National Park Service, which requires professional boatmen to carry large first-aid chests. By unhappy chance Litton had occasion to use his medical supplies while I was traveling with him—one of his young boatmen was injured and had to be taken out of the Canyon.

The boatman was one of a group that set off to investigate Elves' Chasm, a beautiful little grotto bordered with ferns and flowers and located in a stream-fed side canyon at mile 116. The grotto is at the bottom of a deep, twisting slot where narrow shafts of sunlight fall only at high noon. The air is cool and fresh and full of the sound of splashing and tinkling waterfalls. One can climb for half a mile or more up the stream bed, wading through clear, shallow pools. As we were slowly making our way up the slot one of the passengers hurried ahead and reached a spot about 60 feet above us. There he jarred loose an ax-sharp stone, heavy enough to have cleft a man's skull to the teeth.

The stone ricocheted off the walls of the slot, bounced sideways and struck the boatman in the leg between the ankle and knee. Surprisingly, it did not break a bone or cut a major blood vessel; but it gouged out a wound about two inches long, half an inch wide and an inch deep. The boatman, a strong, well-conditioned young man of 22, made no sound. He merely glanced up with a weary expression at the man who kicked loose the rock, and then he sat down beside a pool, plunging his leg into the cool water.

By late afternoon the boatman had been taken out of Elves' Chasm, and we had rejoined the boats. Camp was made a few miles downriver in Conquistador Aisle, where the gorge runs straight for nearly three miles. The water has only light rapids in it and the smooth, pondlike stretches are filled with magnificent reflections of the flaring cliffs above. But the cliffs are insurmountable; there was only one way out for the young boatman—by helicopter. And there was only one way to communicate with the private company that operates helicopters in the Canyon. Thirty-seven miles below Conquistador Aisle the Colorado is joined by Havasu Creek. The Indian reservation, home of Lemuel J. Paya, can be reached from the junction by a 10-mile climb that includes an ascent of the 200-foot cliff at Mooney Falls, where the sailor-prospector dangled for two days before falling to his death. The telephone on the reservation, when the line is not cut by flash floods and rockslides, usually works.

By good fortune there was among Litton's passengers an excellent rock-climber named John Hurst, a professor of psychology at the University of California, who volunteered to make the phone call. A boatman would take him down to the mouth of Havasu Creek next day, and from there Hurst would make his way up the side canyon.

The injured boatman was not in severe pain and soon after dusk he was asleep, lying on the ground beside a low, bushy tamarisk. What happened to him during the night is another illustration of the widespread notion that calamities never come singly.

Scorpions are nocturnal. At full dark one of them emerged from its hiding place, perhaps among the roots of the tamarisk, and commenced its nightly hunting. It crawled across the injured boatman's thigh; he made a sudden motion and the scorpion stung him. The sting, he said, was damned painful, like that of a wasp but a good deal worse. One of the boatman's friends, sleeping nearby, woke up and killed the scorpion. It was slender, straw-colored and about three inches in length including its elongated abdomen or sting-tipped "tail."

In a small book called *Poisonous Dwellers of the Desert,* published by the Southwestern Monuments Association, there is a section on scorpions. "More deaths have occurred in Arizona from scorpion sting than from the bites and stings of all other creatures combined. . . . Of the more than 20 species of scorpions . . . the two deadly forms have been found only across the southern portion of the state and in the bottom of the Grand Canyon." The prose is unduly alarming. The stings of "deadly" scorpions are rarely fatal to adults in average health, although they may be disastrous to those who suffer from heart or lung ailments, and to very young children. The recommended treatment is to apply a tight tourniquet near the puncture point, between it and the heart, and to place a pack of crushed ice on the site of the sting; the tourniquet is removed a few minutes later.

Tourniquets or the material to make them can be found in any first-aid chest. In midsummer, ice in the Canyon would seem to be another matter. In recent years, however, quick-acting cold packs have become available, and Litton carries them. They resemble small plastic pillows, containing about 60 per cent water and 40 per cent ammonium nitrate in pellet form. These ingredients are kept separate by a thin membrane inside the pillow. When the membrane is broken by a squeeze or a blow, the ammonium nitrate and the water combine in a chemical reaction

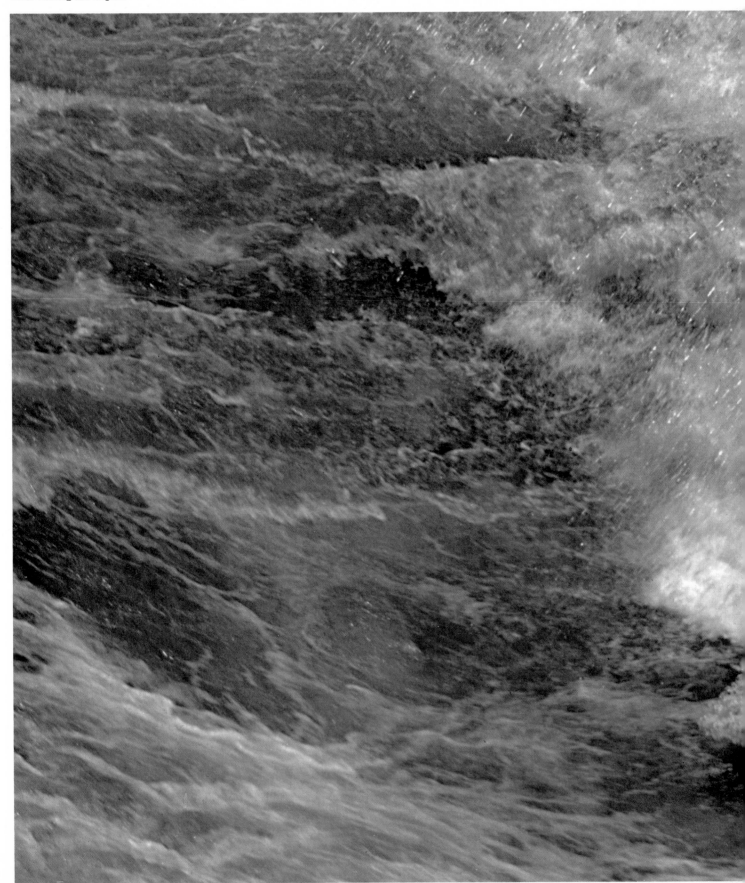

Fighting the river as a towering wave almost swamps his wooden dory, an oarsman confronts Lava Falls Rapids, one of the roughest

stretches of white water on the Colorado River. The dory is one of the few wooden boats that run the river through the Grand Canyon.

that swiftly drops the temperature of the pack well below freezing.

The pack worked well; by morning the pain of the scorpion's sting had almost vanished. The twice-injured boatman still had to wait for the volunteer climber to reach the Indian village and arrange for the rescue, but on the second morning after the boatman's injury a helicopter descended into the gorge, picked him up and carried him to a hospital on the South Rim. He soon recovered and was ready to row his boat on Litton's next trip.

The injured man's place was filled by a trainee oarsman, who had already taken boats through some of the rapids, and the voyage continued. No more scorpions were seen, although each evening when the passengers selected places to make their beds they began to examine nearby driftwood logs, tamarisks and rocks with dark crevices. No more stones were kicked loose by climbers, and when the sun rose like a fiery tomahawk over the rim of the gorge the passengers knew how to combat its heat; they drank from the river, often as much as 10 or 12 pints a day. They began, almost all of them, to move more easily and comfortably in the wilderness. In the absence of artificial light the rhythm of their lives was keyed once more to the turning of the earth, dawn and dusk, sun and stars. The beauty of the Canyon took hold of them and they began to be absorbed in it.

The boats moved on past Tapeats Creek, a cold, rushing tributary stream full of watercress and darting trout; past Deer Creek, which pours out of a narrow cleft high in the Canyon wall and plunges 125 feet to the river below; and slowly they approached the most violent of all the rapids on the river, Lava Falls.

The western part of the Canyon, as noted earlier, was alive with volcanic action about a million years ago. At that time the Canyon had already been created by erosion and probably appeared much as it does today. Then, in a series of violent eruptions, lava burst up through the bed of the river and forced its way out of the walls of the Canyon. From volcanic vents on the northern plateaus red-hot streams of lava poured down over the North Rim into the Canyon, making a dam across the Colorado about 1,400 feet high. The very thought of it caused Major Powell to reach for his exclamation points. "What a conflict of water and fire there must have been here! Just imagine a river of molten rock running down into a river of melted snow. What a seething and boiling of the waters; what clouds of steam rolled into the heavens!"

The lava dam created a lake in the Canyon about 180 miles long. But then the river reduced most of the dam to chunks, to granules, to dust and swept it away, just as it will sweep away all the concrete dams that temporarily vex its course. Traces of the lava dam, which was far more massive and of far more durable material than the structures erected by man, can still be seen along the upper walls of the gorge.

Near mile 178 another relic of the dam, a block of black basalt, rises from the middle of the river. Perched on the rim of the gorge not far away is a cinder cone of a long-dead volcano nearly a mile in diameter, so well preserved that it appears ready to erupt at any moment. The cone, the block and the black hardened lava on the walls lend the gorge a grim aspect appropriate to the rapids roaring there.

Lava Falls, which has caused more upsets than any rapids in the Canyon, is about 80 yards wide and 300 long. On the standard scale of rapids, its rating is somewhere above 10, the most savage white water encountered by boatmen in North America. At its head, stretching across the central third of the river, there is a shelf with a straight drop of 12 feet. To avoid capsizing, boatmen must steer to one side or the other of the shelf; near each bank is an opening where the drop is less severe. But even in the openings there are giant rocks and deep holes and waves that appear large enough to smother any small craft.

Litton assembled his passengers on shore at the head of Lava Falls and made a brief speech. He would never, he said, take a boat through this stretch of water if he could avoid it. Lava Falls Rapids was a beast. I glanced at him, looking for his customary half smile, but it was not there. Previously he had not offered his passengers a choice between riding through rapids and walking around them, but now he did. Indeed he urged them to walk, and the great majority took his advice. However, a half dozen of them remained to try the boats.

I got into Litton's dory and we pushed off into quiet water above the rapids. He steered close to the right bank. Neither of us spoke; the noise of the water would have drowned our voices in any case. We entered Lava Falls at what seemed to me the perfect place and angle; but suddenly the boat plummeted headlong into a deep hole and then pitched upward at an angle of nearly 90 degrees. As the water closed over my head I had a glimpse of Litton still rowing, his oars sweeping the air. In a moment the boat righted itself; then a huge wave broke over it and tipped it so far over on its port side that it seemed certain to capsize. My head was submerged again, and when I could see daylight, Litton had disappeared. The wave had swept him overboard.

The oars were still fastened in the rowlocks. I moved into Litton's place and took them, glancing hopefully left and right to find him. In a moment he bobbed up near the boat. I held out an oar and he seized it, pulling himself up to the gunwale. His bulky life jacket prevented him from climbing back into the boat, even though it was swamped and riding very low in the water; so he hung onto the gunwale as we wallowed along in the rapids. At length he said, "I'll be all right. I'll float down the river, and you try to beach the boat on the right bank."

There were two small sandy beaches on the right, separated by a half-sunken peninsula, a stoneyard of scattered rocks. On the left side of the river there was a heavy torrent of water with four- and five-foot waves: Lower Lava Falls, a continuation of the big rapids. Litton was carried into this while I tried to row cross-current to the right. I could scarcely move the boat, which weighed about 500 pounds empty and a ton when full of water. The current shoved it broadside against the rocks, bounced it over them, and then carried it into quiet water near the second of the beaches, where I pulled it ashore and tied it to the roots of a big tamarisk. Almost 10 minutes later Litton came walking slowly up the riverbank toward me, grinning. "Pleasant day," he said. He had been carried a quarter of a mile downstream and across the river, constantly fighting for breath while the waves broke over him.

The other boats came through the rapids singly at long intervals. Two of them, following the course Litton had taken, had much the same experience. Waves broke over them and knocked men overboard. Two others were tipped upside down; they rolled through Lava Falls with glimpses of their bright red bottom paint showing in the white water. But in every case the oarsmen and passengers were able to catch hold of the boats, hang on and ride them into calm pools. Eventually all of the boats were hauled ashore so that repairs could be made. The damage was surprisingly small, requiring only half a day's work. The river had battered, tossed and overturned the boats as it had so long threatened to do, and the only casualty was a passenger who had chosen to walk around the rapids. He had slipped, caught his foot between two rocks, and mildly sprained his ankle.

There are other rapids below Lava Falls but none that remotely approach it in violence. The river becomes increasingly quiet, slower, flowing mile after mile in solitude, stillness and peace. Beyond mile 200 the Canyon is particularly inaccessible; men very rarely venture there on foot. Golden eagles soar along the high crags and sometimes bighorn sheep can be seen on the cliffs there, warily watching the boats far below. At about mile 240 the river enters Lake Mead, the huge reservoir backed up behind Hoover Dam 115 miles away on the Arizona-Nevada border. Hoover is one of the very few dams of which Litton does not disapprove. It was begun 43 years ago. "At that time," he says, "men built dams to fill a legitimate need—in that case flood control." Litton does not believe that the building of dams to generate greater and greater amounts of electric power fills an equivalent need. "Do you know," he says in a tone of resignation, "do you know what's being done with the power we are generating? Do you know why the wild rivers are being killed? In Las Vegas at the Dunes Hotel there's an electric sign, one electric sign, that costs $6,000 a month to operate, and it pulls enough current to illuminate 3,500 houses." Two dams have been proposed for the interior of Grand Canyon, dams that would submerge most of the route we had just traveled. Litton rummaged in his encyclopedia of knowledge of the Canyon and found the speech Theodore Roosevelt had made about it in 1903. The President visited the South Rim and said he hoped nothing would ever be done "to mar the wonderful grandeur, the sublimity, the great loneliness and beauty of the canyon. Leave it as it is. You cannot improve on it. The ages have been at work on it and man can only mar it. What you can do is keep it for your children, your children's children, and for all who come after you."

The transition from river to lake is made with no perceptible change, except that the current diminishes slightly. But as one looks back upstream, it strikes him that there are few things about the Canyon more dramatic than its ending. The walls of the gorge, which have for so many miles imprisoned the river, suddenly vanish. A huge transverse geologic fault has sunk and dropped them thousands of feet. The Colorado, no longer confined, flows out into the lake, bounded by a flat land of limitless horizon. Looking east one can see a long, high escarpment, the Grand Wash Cliffs, marking the line where the fault lowers the land to the level of the outlying desert. There is a small opening in the Grand Wash Cliffs through which the river issues. But as the boats go farther out onto Lake Mead, it becomes more and more difficult to find the opening, and then it too disappears, and there remains not a trace or hint to suggest that the Grand Canyon exists at all.

The Grandeur of Rock and River

Even for those who know the Canyon well, the first journey down the Colorado River becomes a voyage of discovery. It was all the more so for photographer Ernst Haas: although he had photographed the Canyon from the outer rim and from the air, he was entirely unprepared for the landscape of the Inner Gorge.

Haas started downstream in a wooden rowboat from Lee's Ferry on a day in late May. As he reported afterward, his first impression was of sheer desolation—expanses of rock and water. The high-walled corridor had a raw, primordial look that reminded him of the Biblical account of the creation. The whole world, he thought, might have looked like this just after the Lord had formed the land and the seas, before He graced it with living things.

The photographer's sense of the Canyon's great age was confirmed emphatically by the schist walls of Granite Gorge. Here the cliffs' very texture—a texture that is almost tangible in the photograph on pages 178 and 179—proclaimed their antiquity. The two-billion-year-old rock is dark and dense, roughly fretted and scalloped by the river's ceaseless battering, worn but enduring.

The scale of the gorge proved hard to convey photographically without man-made points of reference. But Haas's reaction to the towering cliffs —his feeling of being trapped and overwhelmed—is captured imaginatively in the picture on page 171. Haas set up his camera at the base of a tree, then shot straight up, through the sparse foliage, into the narrow ribbon of sky far above. In the process, Haas discovered that he did not miss greenery; rather, he appreciated plants all the more for their rarity.

In this stark landscape, nature often seemed to imitate art. A black stone half buried in a sandy beach (page 172) appeared as pure abstract form. Other Haas photographs create the effects of fool-the-eye art. In one of these, shown opposite, a riverside ledge and the rippling water in Marble Canyon blend together so perfectly that it is hard to tell where the rock ends and water begins.

Physically, the 17-day river journey was just as rough—and the living as austere—as the gorge's beauty. But the trip's rigors became endurable and even pleasant. By the time Haas ended his voyage, he had made still another discovery; he had learned how little comfort one really needs to be content.

A LIMESTONE LEDGE, MARBLE CANYON

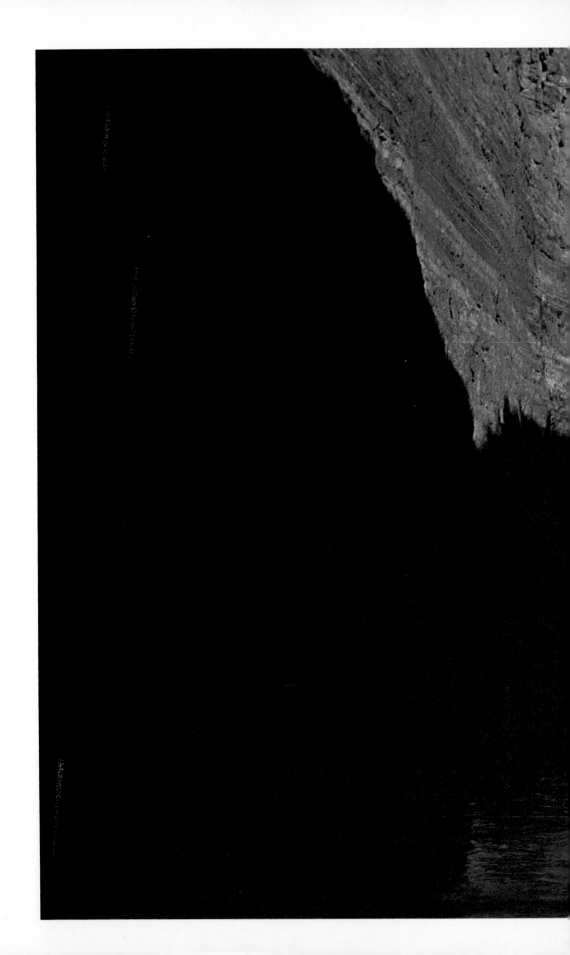

SHADOWS ON THE SOUTH WALL, MARBLE CANYON

SANDSTONE STAINED WITH IRON OXIDES

A TONGUE OF SMOOTH WATER IN RAPIDS

PALISADES OF THE DESERT—A SECTION OF THE SOUTH RIM

ELVES' CHASM, A SIDE CANYON

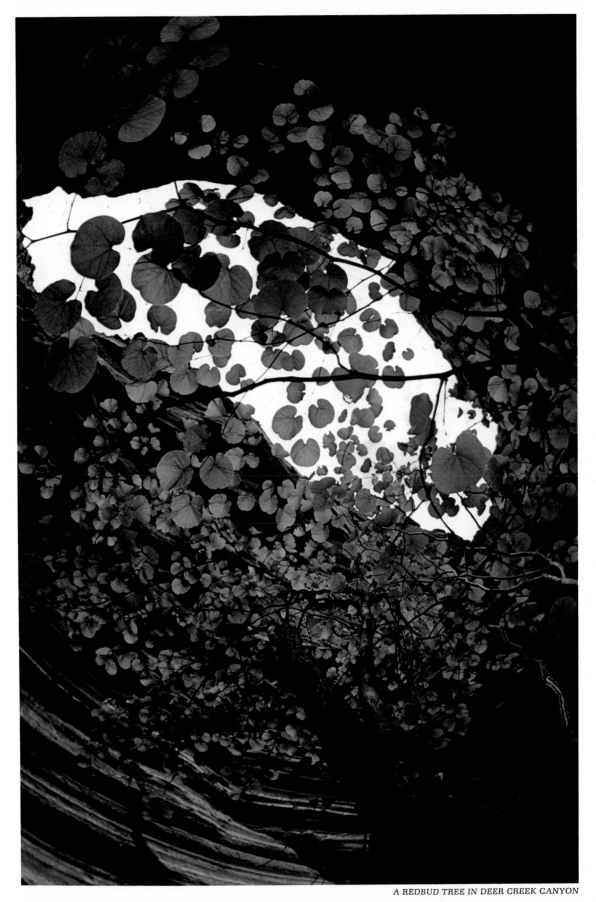

A REDBUD TREE IN DEER CREEK CANYON

ABSTRACT ART IN SAND AND STONE

WHITE BRITTLEBUSH GROWING IN SAND

BOULDERS BESIDE CRYSTAL RAPIDS

WAVES GNAWING AT A LIMESTONE WALL, BUCK FARM CANYON

WHITE WATER, BEDROCK RAPIDS

BEDROCK, TWO BILLION YEARS OLD, AT GRANITE RAPIDS

Bibliography

*Also available in paperback.
†Available in paperback only.

*Braun, Ernest, *Grand Canyon of the Living Colorado*. Sierra Club-Ballantine Books, 1968.

*Darrah, William C., *Powell of the Colorado*. Princeton University Press, 1969.

*Dellenbaugh, Frederick, *A Canyon Voyage*. Yale University Press, 1962.

Dellenbaugh, Frederick, *The Romance of the Colorado River*. Rio Grande Press, 1965.

Fletcher, Colin, *The Man Who Walked through Time*. Knopf, 1967.

*Forrest, Earl R., *The Snake Dance of the Hopi Indians*. Tower Publications, 1961.

Geology and Natural History of the Grand Canyon Region. Fifth Field Conference, Four Corners Geological Society, 1969.

†Hamblin, W. K. and J. R. Murphy, *Grand Canyon Perspectives*. Brigham Young University Printing Service, 1969.

†Hamblin, W. K. and J. K. Rigby, *Guidebook to the Colorado River, Parts 1 and 2*. Brigham Young University Printing Service, 1970.

*Hoffmeister, Donald F., *Mammals of the Grand Canyon*. University of Illinois Press, 1971.

Iliff, Flora G., *People of the Blue Water*. Harper and Brothers, 1954.

*Kluckhohn, Clyde, *Navajo Witchcraft*. Beacon Press, 1962.

Kolb, E. L., *Through the Grand Canyon from Wyoming to Mexico*. Macmillan, 1969.

†Krutch, Joseph Wood, *Grand Canyon, Today and All Its Yesterdays*. William Sloan Associates, 1958.

*Leydet, François, *Time and the River Flowing: Grand Canyon*. Sierra Club-Ballantine Books, 1968.

McDougal, W. B., *Grand Canyon Wild Flowers*. Museum of Northern Arizona, 1964.

†McKee, E. D., R. F. Wilson, W. J. Breed and C. S. Breed, *Evolution of the Colorado River in Arizona*. Northland Press, 1968.

Peattie, Roderick, ed., *The Inverted Mountains: Canyons of the West*. Vanguard Press, 1948.

†Powell, John Wesley, *The Exploration of the Colorado River and Its Canyons*. Dover Publications, 1961.

Rabbitt, M. C., E. D. McKee, C. B. Hunt and L. B. Leopold, *The Colorado River Region and John Wesley Powell*. Geological Survey Professional Paper 669, U.S. Government Printing Office, 1969.

*Scharff, R., ed., *Grand Canyon National Park*. David McKay Company, 1967.

*Simmons, G. C., and D. L. Gaskill, *River Runner's Guide to the Canyons of the Green and Colorado Rivers*. Northland Press, 1969.

*Simmons, Leo W., *Sun Chief, the Autobiography of a Hopi Indian*. Yale University Press, 1970.

Stanton, Robert B., *Down the Colorado*. University of Oklahoma Press, 1965.

Staveley, Gaylord, *Broken Waters Sing*. Little, Brown and Company, 1971.

*Stegner, Wallace, *Beyond the Hundredth Meridian*. Houghton Mifflin and Company, 1954.

Sutton, Ann and Myron, *The Wilderness World of the Grand Canyon*. J. B. Lippincott Company, 1970.

Acknowledgments

The author and editors of this book are particularly indebted to Louise M. Hinchliffe, Curator-Librarian, Grand Canyon National Park, Arizona. They also wish to thank the following: Edmund Andrews, Whittier, California; John Blaustein, Beverly Hills, California; William Bode, Lafayette, California; William J. Breed, Museum of Northern Arizona, Flagstaff; Nellie C. Carico, U.S. Geological Survey, Washington, D.C.; Curtis Chang, Palo Alto, California; Jeff Clayton, Woodland Hills, California; Donald Ducote, Curator of Plants, Arizona-Sonora Desert Museum, Tucson; Joseph G. Hall, Professor of Biology, San Francisco State College; Jon F. Haman, Grand Canyon National Park; W. Kenneth Hamblin, Professor of Geology, Brigham Young University, Provo, Utah; Ron Hayes, Sylmar, California; Warren H. Hill, Grand Canyon National Park; Sidney S. Horenstein, Department of Invertebrate Paleontology, The American Museum of Natural History, New York; George C. Huff, San Rafael, California; J. Donald Hughes, Assistant Professor of History, University of Denver; Merritt Keasey, Curator of Small Animals, Arizona-Sonora Desert Museum, Tucson; Emery Kolb, Grand Canyon, Arizona; Vladimir Kovalik, Pacific Grove, California; Robert Lovegren, Superintendent, Grand Canyon National Park; Otis Dock Marston, Berkeley, California; David C. Ochsner, Grand Canyon National Park; Larry G. Pardue, Plant Information Specialist, New York Botanical Garden; Lemuel J. Paya, Supai, Arizona; Jesse Pogue, Grand Canyon National Park; Walter Rist, Phoenix, Arizona; Ray Rosales, Grand Canyon National Park; Wilbur L. Rusho, Public Information Officer, Bureau of Reclamation, Salt Lake City, Utah; Herbert L. Stahnke, Arizona State University, Tempe; Vernon Taylor, Associate Professor of Geology, Prescott College, Prescott, Arizona; Linda Torgan, Woodland Hills, California; Charlene Vieira, North Rim, Arizona.

Picture Credits

The sources for the pictures in this book are shown below. Credits for the pictures from left to right are separated by commas; from top to bottom they are separated by dashes.

COVER—Josef Muench. Front end papers 1, 2—Philip Hyde. Front end paper 3, page 1—Ernst Haas. 2, 3—James Tallon. 4 through 7—Ernst Haas. 8, 9—Tad Nichols. 14-15—Map by R. R. Donnelley Cartographic Services. 25—Paulus Leeser from *Report upon The Colorado River of the West* by Lieutenant Joseph Christmas Ives, courtesy of Otis Dock Marston Collection, Berkeley, California. 29 through 35—Harald Sund. 41—Ernst Haas. 44, 45—Ernst Haas. 46—Ruth A. Cordner. 50—Map by Margo Dryden. 51—Ernest Braun. 52, 53—Ernest Braun except center Robert Walch. 54—Ernest Braun except top left Bullaty Lomeo. 55—Ernest Braun. 56—Ernest Braun except bottom Bullaty Lomeo. 57—Robert Walch. 58, 59—Ernest Braun. 64, 65—Ernst Haas. 66—Diagrams by Margo Dryden. 71—Ernst Haas. 72, 73—Harald Sund, Ernst Haas. 74, 75—Ernst Haas. 76, 77—Harald Sund. 78, 79—Ernst Haas. 80—Dean Brown. 81—Harald Sund. 82, 83—Ernst Haas. 97, 98, 99—Ernst Haas. 100—Patricia Caulfield. 101—Ernst Haas. 102, 103—Art Kane. 106—United States Department of the Interior, National Park Service, Grand Canyon National Park. 108, 109—Ernst Haas. 119—Paulus Leeser from *The Exploration of the Colorado River and Its Canyons* by J. W. Powell, 1961. 120, 121—Paulus Leeser from *Canyons of the Colorado* by J. W. Powell, 1895. 122—Paulus Leeser from *Exploration of the Colorado River of the West and Its Tributaries,* by J. W. Powell, 1875. 123, 124—Paulus Leeser from *Canyons of the Colorado* by J. W. Powell, 1895. 125 through 128—Paulus Leeser from *Exploration of the Colorado River of the West and Its Tributaries* by J. W. Powell, 1875. 129—Paulus Leeser from *Canyons of the Colorado* by J. W. Powell, 1895. 119 through 129—All courtesy of the United States Department of the Interior, Geological Survey. 139—Tad Nichols. 146—Ernst Haas. 156, 157—Ernst Haas. 163 through 179—Ernst Haas.

Index

Numerals in italics indicate a photograph or drawing of the subject mentioned.